ECONOMIC DISARMAMENT
A STUDY ON INTERNATIONAL COOPERATION

ECONOMIC DISARMAMENT

A STUDY ON INTERNATIONAL COOPERATION

by

J. H. RICHARDSON

M.A. (Cambridge), Ph.D. (London)

*Montague Burton Professor of Industrial Relations in the
University of Leeds. Lately Assistant Chief of Section
Research Division, International Labour Office,
League of Nations, Geneva*

HD
82
.R5
1977

GREENWOOD PRESS, PUBLISHERS
WESTPORT, CONNECTICUT

Library of Congress Cataloging in Publication Data

Richardson, John Henry, 1890–
   Economic disarmament.

   Reprint of the 1931 ed. published by G. Allen & Unwin,
London.
   Includes index.
   1. Economic policy. 2. International cooperation.
3. Tariff. I. Title.
HD82.R5 1977   382.1   77-5720
ISBN 0-8371-9640-X

Originally published in 1931 by George Allen & Unwin Ltd.,
London

Reprinted with the permission of George Allen & Unwin Ltd.

Reprinted in 1977 by Greenwood Press, Inc.

Library of Congress catalog card number   77-5720

ISBN 0-8371-9640-X

Printed in the United States of America

TO
MY FATHER
AND IN MEMORY OF
MY MOTHER

PREFACE

The establishment of peace among the nations involves economic disarmament equally with military, naval, and aerial disarmament. Progress in both fields is dependent on the development of mutual confidence and good will between the peoples of the world, and is the essential preliminary to effective international cooperation.

In recent years much consideration has been given by leading economists and statesmen to methods of removing barriers to world economic progress, and many proposals have been put forward. It is not the purpose of the present volume to advance new solutions for the consideration of experts, but rather to bring together for the convenience of readers with a general interest in the development of international relations some of the chief proposals which are now under discussion, and which will demand attention in the years ahead. The discussion is limited to a few only of the problems which involve conflict and injury from isolated national action, whether by the State or by private organisations. The problems selected are, however, typical and fundamental.

The present need is not so much for the multiplication of plans as for the application of the main features of those already made, many of which are far in advance of measures for their practical realisation. At the same time, with the continuous evolution of economic and political life, no rigid hard-and-fast solution would be effective; there must be constant adaptation to the new requirements of the future.

During the last nine years the writer has had opportunity, as a member of the Research Staff of the International Labour Office of the League of Nations, to study from an international angle the problems which arise, and to observe the first tentative steps taken by the institutions of the League towards economic disarmament and cooperation in place of conflict. This study has confirmed him in the opinion that the interests of humanity will be well served by the progressive removal of barriers to international economic cooperation. Their removal would permit of a more rapid increase in standards of living and would make a considerable contribution to the establishment of world peace.

There are undoubtedly many difficulties, especially those due to exaggerated nationalism and vested interests, but a better understanding of the problems and the importance of their solution will strengthen public opinion in support of measures of disarmament and of constructive cooperation, both between States and private organisations, in the world economic field. It is in the hope of making some contribution to this evolution that the present volume has been written.

It is a pleasing duty to express my thanks to Sir Arthur Salter and Professor J. H. Jones for reading the manuscript and for many valuable suggestions, and to Mr. H. B. Butler for useful criticisms of the chapter on the international regulation of labour standards. To my wife I am specially indebted for continuous help and advice.

J. H. RICHARDSON

The University, Leeds
    March 1931

CONTENTS

ECONOMIC DISARMAMENT
A STUDY ON INTERNATIONAL COOPERATION

CHAPTER I

INTRODUCTION

The post-war years have been marked by a severe struggle in the economic field, as also in the political, between the opposing forces of nationalism and of international cooperation, and, after a decade of conflict, the result, so vital for the future of mankind, is still in doubt.

Economic nationalism was greatly intensified by the war; it was also strengthened by recognition in the Peace Treaties of national claims involving the formation of new States and the changing of frontiers. During the war, many established channels of international trade were diverted or broken, and consequently industries were developed in various countries to manufacture goods hitherto imported. These industries, menaced with destruction by foreign competition after the war, demanded and usually obtained protection by means of tariff barriers. Also, fear of war led many States to desire and take steps to attain economic independence.

It is not difficult under present conditions of production and trade to find arguments in support of certain measures of protection. A State may find it desirable to safeguard its industries against unfair competition from abroad. Thus protection may sometimes be justified against organised dumping, the importation

of subsidised foreign products, or the competition of
goods produced by sweated labour; it is not easy,
however, to obtain the desired protection free from
counterbalancing disadvantages. Again, a country in
an early stage of industrial development may with
advantage foster the growth of its industries until they
are well established. No State can remain satisfied
that its people be merely "hewers of wood and drawers
of water" for others. For the full development of
any people a wide range of skilled occupations is
necessary.

For a State to go beyond such objects and to ensure
by continued protective measures or subsidies the
production of goods at home which could be produced
more efficiently and cheaply abroad, is to throw away
the advantages of foreign trade, lower the general
standard of living and reduce the benefits to be derived
from improvements in transportation. This course,
it is true, may be justified by those who hold the view
that war is inevitable, and that the danger of war
demands national self-sufficiency. But national self-
sufficiency is a deceptive ideal for all but a few
countries. The United States of America, Russia,
possibly the British Empire, conceivably Germany
and France, might pursue it. For most countries
attempts to attain self-sufficiency for war could not
succeed and would involve economic injury to themselves and to other States, although this is not a
decisive argument against the protection of a few
industries which are especially important for war.
Those who believe that civilisation has reached
the stage when war can be eliminated, regard the

measures usually taken to ensure national self-sufficiency as not merely wasteful, but as a fruitful cause of international friction.

DEVELOPMENT OF INTERNATIONAL ECONOMIC ORGANISATION

The forces of economic nationalism, therefore, have not remained unchallenged. A widespread determination to do everything possible to eliminate causes of war has manifested itself in recent years, and has found expression especially in the League of Nations. Being an organisation set up to promote international cooperation, the League has inevitably been called upon to deal with economic problems. Since, however, quarrels and disputes between States are often the direct or indirect consequence of economic conditions, the League's economic work is consistent with its main purpose of maintaining the peace of the world. Indeed, economic disarmament and the development of international cooperation in the fields of production, commerce, finance, and labour have come to be recognised as among the major functions of the League. The need for such action in these fields is implicit in the Covenant of the League, while the Labour provisions of the Peace Treaties state explicitly that "conditions of labour exist involving such injustice, hardship, and privation to large numbers of people as to produce unrest so great that the peace and harmony of the world are imperilled"; the International Labour Organisation was therefore established as an autonomous institution of the League for the purpose of removing such underlying causes of war.

But these official institutions are by no means the only instruments working for the removal of barriers to closer international economic cooperation.[1] Not only the diplomats of different States but also their business men and workers now meet much more frequently than ever before for joint discussion of questions of international interest. In the year after the war the International Chamber of Commerce was formed, to provide a channel for the expression of opinion of the business world with a view to developing cooperation between the nations and removing causes of economic disputes. It thus aims at making a contribution towards the maintenance of peace. This has led to its effective association with the economic work of the League of Nations.

In the field of labour the workers have developed important international organisations which seek to remove unfair conditions of employment. Chief among these is the International Federation of Trade Unions, with headquarters at Amsterdam, which actively supports the objects for which the International Labour Organisation was established; it has also formulated a comprehensive economic policy as basis for national and international action.[2] In addition, there are international federations of workers' unions for each of the chief industries. Employers of labour are represented by the International Organisation of

[1] *The Handbook of International Organisations*, published by the League of Nations, gives information on the objects and activities of all the chief official and unofficial international non-profit-making organisations, including those which deal with economic subjects.
[2] *The Economic Policy of the International Federation of Trade Unions*, Amsterdam, 1929.

Industrial Employers, which also is closely associated with the work of the International Labour Organisation.

These various official and private bodies are non-profit-making. But the wastefulness of intense international competition has led to the formation of a number of international trusts and cartels, which coordinate production and commerce for profit-making purposes. An important example of such a cartel is the International Steel Agreement, in which the chief steel-producing countries of continental Europe are associated. Similar international agreements regulate the production of, or trade in, other commodities, while international trusts, i.e. giant businesses which have acquired a dominant position in world trade, have been built up in a number of industries, including petroleum, tobacco, and matches. International cartels and trusts, and also other forms of industrial agreements, are likely to increase in importance in the future, and may make a considerable contribution to world peace by removing the conflict of unregulated competition.

On financial questions important informal conversations have recently been held between the representatives of the central banks of different countries to develop coordinated international action in the place of a conflict of national policies. The continuation of these conversations is now facilitated by the meetings of the Board of Management of the Bank for International Settlements, and will serve as a complement to the coordinating work in financial matters of the League of Nations.

This enumeration is sufficient to indicate some of

B

the chief means for securing progress in economic disarmament and developing international cooperation.

PROBLEMS TO BE SOLVED

During the early post-war years, international action was concerned mainly with clearing from the path of economic progress obstacles for which the war was directly responsible. First, there was the termination of the war blockades, the feeding of starving populations in disorganised districts, and the reconstruction of devastated areas. Then came a tangle of financial obstacles, including uncertainty about reparation payments, war debts, failure of various States to balance their budgets, and the consequent chaos of currency depreciation.

These problems, the solving of which was essential to economic recovery, demanded chief consideration during the first post-war decade. However, with the gradual removal of these relatively temporary barriers, more fundamental questions began to claim increasing attention. While the closing years of the decade saw currency stability largely restored in most countries, reparations and war debt payments adjusted, and public finances convalescent, a number of important problems remained unsolved.

Chief among these are the tariff question, cut-throat competition for markets between producers in different States, and the relation between such competition and labour conditions; there are also important unsolved problems of currency and finance, especially that of ensuring economy in the use of the world's supply of gold, so that industry and commerce will not be hampered by shortage.

The menace of tariffs has already been indicated, while that of intense unregulated competition for markets is so obvious as to require no emphasis, except in its unfavourable reactions on conditions of labour. Thus demands for wage reductions and maintenance of long hours of labour are often supported by the argument that these measures are necessary owing to the low standards of working conditions in competing countries. Also a lowering of the standard in one country which gains a competitive advantage is followed by similar changes in rival countries. On the other hand, a country which desires to raise its labour conditions is hampered by low standards abroad. These reactions tend to develop ill-feeling between the workers in different countries, while hardship and privation result in social unrest, and both are a menace to world peace.

In the monetary field there is danger that the central banks of the different countries may each endeavour to build up large gold reserves without taking account of the general world situation. Some countries have already pursued this policy during recent years. Such a scramble for the limited supplies of gold available for monetary reserves results in scarcity. As a consequence there is a shortage of currency to meet the needs of industry and commerce, and the level of prices tends to decline. This is an important cause, though by no means the only cause, of industrial depression, accompanied by unemployment, and international competition is rendered more severe. To avoid these dangers, international cooperation between the chief central banks is necessary to ensure economy in the use of gold and coordination of monetary policy.

These questions of tariffs, intense competition for markets, labour standards, and monetary stability are the main issues to be faced in the field of international economic relations during the next decade. To attempt their solution by clear-cut measures and precipitate haste would be to court failure. The complicated structure of the modern economic world demands gradual evolution rather than sudden change.

The vital question, however, is what direction the evolution will take, and upon the answer depends whether the future will see a succession of wars or the maintenance of peace. In international affairs the dominance of economic relations is steadily increasing. These relations may be used either as a basis for peace or as a cause of conflict. True, the economic interests of different States are sometimes divergent. On the other hand, there are many common interests the development of which would contribute to the conciliation of those which are conflicting. On these lines the British Committee on Industry and Trade express the view that, as a matter not of sentiment but of business, "our major interest as a country is identical with and not opposed to the major interest of the countries which buy our products and supply our needs". They also consider that "it is, in the long run, much more important for British trade that the purchasing power of the countries with which that trade is carried on shall be revived and increased, than that British exporters should profit by adverse conditions affecting some of their competitors to displace them from some particular market".[1]

Those who hold the view that the chief underlying causes of war in the modern world are economic will recognise the urgent necessity for States to adopt a policy of economic disarmament and cooperation. The more States attempt to become self-contained economic units, the greater will be the danger of conflict. A State which erects high tariff barriers round its home market increases its difficulties in securing markets abroad. Its desire for larger markets can hardly fail to stimulate demand for territorial aggrandisement.

Many writers strongly protest that expansion of political frontiers does not contribute to the prosperity of a people.[2] This view seems to be well-founded if international trade is not unduly hampered by tariff and other restrictions. If such restrictions become excessive, however, there will tend to be pressure for territorial expansion in order to secure the economic advantages of a larger free trade area. The statements that "political and military power can in reality do nothing for trade", and that "the individual merchants and manufacturers of small nations, exercising no such power, compete successfully with those of the great"[3] are true only on the assumption that conditions of trade between States are reasonably fair and unrestricted.

Facilities for international trade are being steadily developed by improvements in transportation and rapidity of communication. These factors are tending greatly to increase international interdependence and

---

[1] *Final Report*, London, 1929.
[2] See especially Norman Angell, *The Great Illusion*, London, 1914.
[3] *Ibid.*, Synopsis, p. ix.

are definitely contributing to the breaking down of national rivalries. They may, indeed, be decisive factors in the conflict between economic nationalism and international cooperation. It should be recognised, however, that the erection of economic barriers to trade seriously detracts from the advantages accruing from improvements in transportation. It is absurd that many of the benefits which mankind could derive from real technical progress in transportation should be withheld by the construction of artificial obstacles.

There is a wide measure of international agreement that such obstacles should be swept aside. Economists, while calling attention to the complicated technical problems involved, have found little difficulty in indicating the main lines to be followed. But so great have been the forces of political suspicion and distrust and so powerful the vested interests that little progress in economic disarmament has yet been made.

LINES OF PROGRESS

The World Economic Conference convened by the League of Nations in 1927, and representative of Governments, industrialists, workers, traders, and economists, called attention to the harmful effects upon production and trade which result from high and constantly changing tariffs, and to the improvements which could be obtained by increased facilities for trade and commerce. It therefore declared that "the time has come to put an end to increase in tariffs and to move in the opposite direction". It also indicated the advantages to be obtained from agreements between producers in different countries to eliminate the strain and injury of unfair competition for markets.

Yet more than two years later speaker after speaker at the 1929 Assembly of the League reiterated that States had shown little inclination to give effect to the recommendations of the World Economic Conference, and that the situation was even worse than when the Conference was held. The Assembly therefore urged that definite measures should be taken with a view to agreement against further tariff increases as a preliminary step to reductions. An attempt to secure such an agreement was made at the Tariff Truce Conference which met in Geneva in February 1930, but difficulties were encountered and little progress was made.

It was at the 1929 Assembly also that M. Briand launched the idea of a United States of Europe.[1] The post-war prosperity of the United States of America had contrasted greatly with the economic crises and depressions which many European countries had experienced. Europe had therefore made every endeavour to read the riddle of American prosperity. While this prosperity could be explained by no single factor, it was generally agreed that an important element was the existence of a large territory without economic barriers. Europe, with its many divisions and economic obstacles, is in marked contrast, and nowhere is the need for economic disarmament greater.[2] This may be

[1] Many features of this proposal resemble those which have been advocated for several years by the Pan-European Union.
[2] The Tariff Truce Conference (Geneva 1930) was for practical purposes a European conference, since it was attended by delegates from twenty-seven European and only three other States; several extra-European countries, however, sent observers.

facilitated by the geographical contiguity of the States, and by the fact that many of them are at approximately the same stage of industrial development. It is the lack of these conditions which renders difficult the establishment, now so much discussed, of a common economic policy for the British Commonwealth.

In attempting the achievement of European economic unity, one warning is necessary. It would be unfortunate if this unity were developed in such a manner as to involve hostility to other parts of the world. True, the United States of America has erected high tariff barriers against the manufactures of other countries, but it is very doubtful whether she derives advantage from these barriers now that her industries are so highly developed. Her *general* prosperity, though not the prosperity of certain of her industries, seems now quite independent of her tariff policy. The same warning applies equally to proposals for coordinating the economic policy of the various parts of the British Commonwealth. The advantages which would accrue from such a coordination would be likely to be more than counterbalanced if economic armaments were constructed against the rest of the world.

Economic disarmament, by means of trusts and cartels, has already made progress in some industries, but in others cut-throat competition is still the rule and is an underlying cause of international ill-will. This competition is often marked by the employment of such devices as subsidies, export bounties, and transportation facilities, designed to give the producers of the country an advantage over their foreign rivals. The interests of world peace and harmonious economic

progress demand that such methods should not be
applied, but that instead cooperation between producers and also consumers in different countries
should be developed. In some industries the self-interest
of the producers may stimulate them to establish
cooperation on their own initiative; in others the
Economic Organisation of the League of Nations may
usefully help by calling attention to the causes and
consequences of excessive international competition,
and by facilitating discussions and the establishment
of cooperation between all those interested not only
as producers but as consumers. There is, for example,
a possibility that cooperation between coal producers
in different countries may develop from the investigation which the Economic Committee of the League is
conducting into the causes and effects of the present
difficulties confronting the coal industry.

Progress in ensuring reasonable standards of labour
conditions in different countries is the task of the
International Labour Organisation.[1] During the first
post-war decade the Conference of the Organisation
was successful in adopting about thirty international
conventions, and these led to some four hundred acts
of ratification by the various States. The Conventions
deal with a wide range of subjects, including hours
of work, minimum age of employment, compensation
for industrial accidents and diseases, and sickness
insurance; a considerable number of conventions
deal with special classes of workers, e.g. dockers,
seamen, bakers, and also women and young persons.

[1] See the Preamble to the Labour Provisions of the Treaties of
Peace.

The wage question, however, has hitherto received little attention from the Conference. In 1928 a Convention and a Recommendation on Minimum Wage-Fixing Machinery were adopted, but these are very modest, and are likely to affect the conditions of only a small number of workers in the different countries. Yet the wage question is a fundamental issue. Wages, more than other conditions of labour, are affected by international competition, and low wage standards in certain countries are formidable weapons in international commerce. Also, countries may improve their hours of labour and other working conditions at the expense of wages. Consequently the ratification of conventions on hours and other conditions may represent only a very limited progress in the improvement of labour standards. In order, therefore, to ensure that economic warfare shall not be carried on by means of unfair competition in labour standards, it is essential that the International Labour Organisation should secure the adoption and application of agreements providing for the establishment of reasonable levels of wages in the different countries. This development is a necessary complement to the establishment of reasonable standards for hours and other conditions.

The main line of progress in monetary policy is towards greater stability of prices and productive activity. The economic and financial advisers of governments and central banks in the chief industrial countries are aware of the close relation between currency requirements and industrial prosperity. But the volume of currency is once more intimately related to the gold reserves. In pre-war days the automatic

operation of the gold standard was among the chief
factors responsible for fluctuations in industrial prosperity and social welfare. It contributed to booms of
intense production followed by crises and depression,
while long-period changes in the value of gold also
increased the risks of industry and commerce. It is
true that the restoration of the gold standard in some
countries and the adoption of the gold exchange and
bullion standards in others has resulted in a high degree
of monetary stability when compared with the widely
fluctuating values of paper currencies in the early post-
war years. Still greater stability is, however, desirable
in order to avoid undue variations in industrial activity.
The weights and measures used in industry and commerce have long been invariable, whereas the monetary
unit is yet subject to considerable fluctuations.

Many countries having adopted gold as a basis for
their currency, each is affected by the monetary policy
of the others. Independent national action is therefore
likely to disturb the monetary conditions and economic
development of other countries. Only by international
cooperation between the leading industrial countries
can these consequences be avoided.

The problem is admittedly difficult. As indicated
earlier, progress has been made by cooperation between
the central banks of a number of countries, including
the United States of America and Great Britain. This
cooperation is likely to be facilitated by the regular
meeting of representatives of central banks in the
administration of the Bank for International Settlements. The question is also being investigated by
the Financial Organisation of the League of Nations.

Economic disarmament would achieve notable progress if the various States would recognise that the best interests of each would be served in the monetary field not by continuing independent action but by the adoption of a coordinated international policy.

The problems discussed above are by no means the only ones involving international economic conflict.[1] The question of migration in relation to overcrowded countries and sparsely populated countries is a source of international friction, and the restrictions imposed by some States are resented by others. Conflict arises in attempts to secure monopolistic control of mineral resources and other raw materials, e.g. oil, copper, rubber, and of transportation routes in the interests of the nationals of one or a few countries. International friction is caused if such monopolistic power is used differentially to the disadvantage of some countries. Financial power is often used internationally to strengthen the position of some countries against others. Thus loans made to the Governments of small countries by powerful lenders in one or other of the great financial centres may be used in the narrow political and economic interests of the country from which the loan is made. Such action constitutes a menace to rival countries and provokes retaliation.[2] In these and in many other ways States continue to build up economic armaments against one another.

[1] For recent accounts of various aspects of economic conflict, see *The Economic War*, by the Hon. George Peel, London, 1930, and *The World's Economic Dilemma*, by E. M. Patterson, London, 1930.
[2] This form of friction would be avoided if international loans were made on similar lines to the Austrian and other loans under the financial reconstruction schemes of the League of Nations.

The present volume deals only with the four fundamental problems of tariffs, unregulated competition, labour standards and currency in the field of international relations. They are typical examples of international economic conflict, and are likely to be much to the fore during the next decade. Progress toward their solution would facilitate economic disarmament in other fields. Of these four problems only the main features and the general direction of progress towards economic disarmament and international cooperation are reviewed; to attempt a detailed survey would demand at least a separate volume for each problem.

The whole argument is based on the assumption that international cooperation in the economic field is in the best interest of the peoples of the world, and that its advantages can be obtained without in any way sacrificing the benefits of healthy competition. It is frankly admitted that the forces of ultra-nationalism within each country are powerful and tenacious, while the practical measures of progress which any country may propose are largely limited by the extent of the advance which other countries are prepared to make. The writer is of opinion that the lines of world development lead in the direction of economic disarmament and international cooperation, and that either now or ultimately they will be followed. But it is urgent that progress shall not be delayed if the present or especially immediately succeeding generations are to be safeguarded against war. The achievement of this progress is one of the important contributions which the present generation can make to human welfare.

CHAPTER II

TARIFF BARRIERS TO INTERNATIONAL TRADE

Distrust and hostility between nations find their bitterest economic expression in international trade relations. The terminology of war is openly used; markets are attacked and conquered; the home market must be defended against foreign invasion; tariff wars are conducted by means of discriminations, retaliations, and fighting tariffs (*tarifs de combat*), while trade is hampered by barriers and prohibitions. In this atmosphere of conflict the mutual advantages of international trade to producer and consumer are largely overlooked.

Obstacles to international trade tend to be most numerous and difficult during periods of intense nationalism and of international political antagonism. Thus the free trade movement during the middle of the nineteenth century was succeeded, in the generation preceding 1914, by a series of tariff wars and tariff increases which were the economic counterpart of the growth of military and naval armaments. The rise in tariff levels might even be regarded as an index of the nationalist sentiment which culminated in the outbreak of war.

The heritages of the World War have included exaggerated nationalism, suspicion, and distrust, together with economic chaos, and it is therefore not surprising to find that tariff barriers are now higher, more complex, and unstable than before the war.[1] Also

[1] *The World Economic Conference, Final Report*, League of Nations, C.E.I. 44 (1), Geneva, 1927.

the upward movement has not yet been arrested. The most recent official statistics comparing tariff levels in different countries are for the year 1925, prepared by the League of Nations for the World Economic Conference, Geneva, 1927[1]. They show the tariff levels in 1925 and also the increases over the levels in 1913 to have been especially great for manufactured goods. Since 1925, however, the position has been largely modified by increases of tariffs on agricultural products. For manufactured goods the tariff levels in 1925, calculated in percentages of the value of the goods) were as follows:

Country	Tariff level, per cent.
Great Britain, Netherlands	under 10
Denmark, Switzerland	10 to 15
Austria, Belgium, India, Sweden	15 to 20
Canada, France, Germany, Italy, Yugoslavia	20 to 25
Argentine, Australia, Czechoslovakia, Hungary	25 to 30
Poland	30 to 35
Spain, United States of America	over 35

During the period 1925 to 1930, the general tendency was for the raising of tariff levels. Even during the year following the World Economic Conference in May 1927, which adopted recommendations in favour of greater liberty of trading especially by tariff reductions, tariffs were increased in several

[1] *Tariff Level Indices*, League of Nations, Economic and Financial Section, Geneva, 1927 (C.E.I. 37), pages 15–17. In addition to giving indices of tariff levels, this memorandum describes the problems and methods of measuring tariff levels. These are also discussed by A. Loveday in a Paper on "The Measurement of Tariff Levels," *Journal of the Royal Statistical Society*, Part IV, 1929.

countries, although there is evidence that the work of the Conference served to restrain the upward movement. There were further increases in protectionism in certain countries during the years 1928–1930, while no reductions of any real value for developing greater liberty in international trade were made.[1] Important changes during the last four years include tariff increases by France, Poland, Bulgaria, the United States of America, China, Canada, Australia, and, especially on cotton goods, by India. The most recent changes have been in overseas countries; European States have made comparatively few changes for manufactured goods during the last two years, although there has been a tendency to raise the duties on agricultural products.

Tariff agreements between different European States are still concluded for short periods, often not exceeding one year, and this increases the uncertainty of international trade relations; the present duration of agreements compares unfavourably with that before the war, when the usual period was about ten years.

Tariff barriers of greater height, complexity, and instability than before the war are not the only obstacles to the development of international trade. The post-war years have been marked also by serious prohibitions of importation and exportation of certain commodities and by export duties; international trade has been diverted into artificial channels by production

[1] League of Nations Economic Organisation, Consultative Committee, *Application of the Recommendations of the International Economic Conference*, Reports on the periods May 1927 to May 1929 (C.C.E. 7 and C. 130. M. 45. 1929. II). These Reports give detailed analyses of tariff changes in the various countries.

subsidies and bounties on exportation, and has been hampered by obstructions to transportation.[1] Progress in the removal of some of these obstacles has been achieved during recent years, but tariffs have continued to rise and constitute the chief barrier to trade. They therefore receive special attention in the present and the two following chapters.

CAUSES OF HIGH POST-WAR TARIFFS

A chief cause of high tariffs since the war is the strength of nationalist sentiment in various countries to which successful appeal has been made by industries desiring protection. These industries have emphasised and exploited the desire for a high degree of national economic self-sufficiency. This desire is largely a consequence of the post-war feeling of insecurity which has prevailed especially in many countries of continental Europe. Industries important for purposes of national defence have been fostered. Also other national industries formerly of small scale have succeeded in securing high protection and have expanded their production to supply the needs of the home market, often with a surplus for exportation. This policy of high protection has been pursued particularly by Poland, Czechoslovakia, and other new States created by the Peace Treaties. Yet many of the

[1] Details of obstacles to international trade are given in the *Final Report of the Trade Barriers Committee of the International Chamber of Commerce*, submitted to the World Economic Conference, Geneva, 1927, League of Nations, C.E.I. 5 (1). Many of the proposals of the International Chamber of Commerce for the removal of these obstacles were adopted by the World Economic Conference, see *Final Report*, C.E.I. 44 (1).

countries which practise high protection are so small that the attempt to secure self-sufficiency is costly, involving a lower standard of living than would be possible if the advantages of freer international trade were enjoyed, and is doomed to failure.

High tariffs have also been established to protect industries which expanded artificially during the war when foreign supplies were not available. These industries would often have been unable to maintain themselves if exposed to the full force of international competition on the resumption of trade relations after the war. This would have involved for these industries loss of capital and reduced employment which have been avoided by tariffs to ensure their protection in the home market.

Development of large-scale industry, often with the protection of tariff barriers, has led to the need for wider markets. These have sometimes been secured, either to dispose of a temporary surplus or on a more permanent basis, by the process of dumping abroad. The practice of dumping has been especially prevalent during the post-war years.[1] Protection has consequently been demanded and often obtained by industries which have been adversely affected by the competition of dumped goods.

High tariffs have also resulted from ineffective tariff bargaining. High rates have often been introduced for the purpose of bargaining with other countries by making considerable reductions in return for reciprocal

[1] See *Memorandum on Dumping*, by Jacob Viner, Professor of Political Economy at Chicago University, submitted to the Preparatory Committee of the International Economic Conference, League of Nations document C.E.C.P. 36 (1), Geneva 1926, pp. 7–8.

advantages. Frequently, however, the negotiations have been less successful than had been anticipated, and, in consequence, the tariffs actually applied have been higher than was intended.

Another cause of high post-war tariffs has been the disturbance to international trade by depreciating currencies. The effect of depreciation is to give an artificial stimulus to the exportation of goods from the countries practising currency inflation, and other countries have established protective tariffs against these goods. With the cessation of currency inflation by almost all countries there is a tendency to withdraw the special measures of protection introduced during the periods of depreciation.

GENERAL ECONOMIC ADVANTAGES OF FREEDOM OF INTERNATIONAL TRADE

There is general agreement about the mutual advantages of international trade. Some countries are relatively more efficient than others in the production of certain commodities. This is due to natural resources, climate, geographical position, and the qualities of the population in scientific progress, management, and workmanship. The volume of goods produced and the material standard of living of the peoples of the world will be greatest if each country uses its capital and labour in producing those commodities in which it has relatively high efficiency, and then exchanges part of its products for those of other countries. Each country will benefit by the exchange, although by superior commercial skill or by the exercise of monopolistic power some countries may secure a disproportionate share of the advantages of international trade.

Subject to qualifications which will be examined later, the establishment of tariff barriers diverts capital and labour into less productive channels and therefore reduces the world's income. The reduction may affect some countries more than others in consequence of their greater dependence on foreign trade. Thus a country which can produce a wide variety of goods with reasonable efficiency is less dependent on international trade than a country which has only a limited range of products. Small countries, therefore, tend to lose more than large ones from interference with the free course of international trade. The United States of America, which includes such a wide variety of climatic conditions and natural resources and has so large an internal market, is injured far less by a high tariff policy than are the smaller customs units of Europe.

The losses due to high national tariffs are also greater as facilities increase for the transport of goods and as large-scale production develops. They now inflict much greater injury to standards of living than in the early years of the nineteenth century before the progress of rail and ocean transportation. Improved transportation served to break down the local *octroi* which hampered trade between the districts within different countries a century ago, and the further developments of the twentieth century may well contribute to the removal of artificial barriers to international trade.

Use of the capital and labour of a country in the production of goods and services in which it is relatively more efficient than other countries implies free-

dom for imports as well as for exports. Yet imports
are often looked upon with disfavour. It is thought
that by importing goods an advantage is conferred
upon the foreigner and that this involves an injury at
home. Therefore, although the free-traders' argument
that imports are paid for by exports has never been
refuted, barriers are frequently erected against imports
without considering their effect either on the cost of
living of the consumer or on the production of goods
for export. "It is too often overlooked that the attempt
to stimulate artificially industries which would not
otherwise flourish in a country may check the development of those industries for which it is naturally
suited. Nations may determine, for political or other
reasons, that it is essential for their safety to develop
increased self-sufficiency, but it is appropriate . . . to
point out that this has in most cases involved a sacrifice
of material prosperity. In such cases, the loss is borne
by consumers, who have to pay more for the products
of the protected industry, and by those engaged in
the industries that would otherwise have a larger
possibility of export."[1]

The argument that imports are paid for by exports
is subject to qualification; evidently a country may have
an excess of imports or an excess of exports. This
often results in an increase or decrease of capital within
the country; but the problem of investment policy
and the relative advantages of investing capital at
home or abroad should be decided independently from
tariff policy.

[1] *World Economic Conference, Final Report,* League of Nations
document C.E.I. 44 (1), p. 29.

It is, of course, true that when a country establishes
or increases tariffs it inflicts injury on other countries.
This is harmful to international relations and often
involves economic conflict. A recent example is the
high tariff applied by the United States in July 1930
which caused much bitterness abroad. In such circumstances other countries tend to raise tariffs, either to
inflict an injury in retaliation or in the hope of securing
concessions by bargaining. They appear to hold the
view that to inflict an injury on the foreigner must
confer a benefit on the home country. They bargain
for the maximum reduction in return for the minimum
concession. They fail to realise that a retaliatory
tariff almost inevitably causes injury to themselves
by further increasing the maldistribution of their
capital and labour. Also, experience has shown that
bargaining tariffs are often unsuccessful in securing
the desired concessions and their effect is to distort
still more the natural course of production and
trade.[1]

The chief supporters of tariffs are producers for the
the home market who are exposed to the competition
of goods from abroad. If producers in a single home
market industry can secure a tariff they clearly derive
benefit from its protection; they can raise prices and
increase production. If the industry is subject to increasing returns, i.e. if its cost of production per unit
falls as output increases, it may even ultimately develop

[1] An account of the chief methods of conducting tariff negotiations
is given by Mr. W. T. Page in a *Memorandum on European Bargaining Tariffs*, submitted to the Preparatory Committee of the
World Economic Conference, League of Nations document C.E.C.P.
97, Geneva, 1927.

an export trade based on high selling prices in the protected home market and low prices abroad.[1] The more industries, however, that secure protection, the smaller is the gain of each since the benefits they derive as producers are more and more counterbalanced by the higher prices they pay as consumers of goods produced by other protected industries. The loss from tariffs falls most heavily on the ordinary consumer and also on industries producing for foreign markets, which find their costs of production increased.

Once tariffs are established the vested interests of the protected industries make it difficult to reduce or abolish the duties. The industries point to the loss of capital and employment which will result from the withdrawal of protection. The gain to consumers from lower prices and to exporters from lower costs seems more remote and less tangible. Also, consumers are usually unorganised and much less vocal than the vested interests affected by a proposal for lowering protective duties. A sudden large reduction of protective tariffs would of course inflict loss of capital and employment on the industries concerned. Therefore, reductions should be effected gradually by small amounts; this would largely, if not altogether, avoid capital losses and would facilitate the transference of labour. The process of reduction would be facilitated both politically and economically if successive reductions were made simultaneously in a number of countries.

[1] Dumping abroad at prices lower than selling prices at home, and especially at prices below cost of production, greatly intensifies international competition and is a fruitful cause of economic conflict.

Objects for which Tariffs may be Imposed

Some of the reasons for which tariffs may be imposed have already been indicated in the section on causes of high post-war tariffs. The chief objects will be examined here with special reference to their economic value. Many of them are indicated in the title of the United States of America Tariff Act, dated June 17, 1930, the purpose of which is "to provide revenue, to regulate commerce with foreign countries, to encourage the industries of the United States, to protect American labour, and for other purposes".[1] Expressed somewhat more fully, tariffs are usually established with one or more of the following objects:

(1) provision of revenue,

(2) maintenance of industries considered essential or desirable,

(3) protection of infant industries,

(4) prevention of unfair foreign competition,

(5) to afford preference to the products of certain countries,

(6) bargaining or retaliation.

A tariff for revenue purposes should be considered primarily as a form of taxation and not as a measure of protection. Its incidence should be determined as

---

[1] Its authors might have added: to withhold many of the benefits of international trade from the American consumer, to hinder the growth of the American export trade and to arouse antagonism abroad. Actually the high level of the new tariff created much bitterness in many countries. For example, in Switzerland the question of boycotting goods from the United States was seriously advocated by industrialists and Chambers of Commerce, and the Swiss Government was urged to raise duties in retaliation.

closely as possible and its value judged in relation to the general scheme of taxation. Usually the burden is borne mainly by the home consumers. The most suitable commodities on which to impose a tariff for revenue purposes are those not produced at home or on which a corresponding excise is levied on home production. Otherwise, revenue is reduced by production within the country instead of importing from abroad. In proportion as protection is afforded to the home producer the value of the tariff for revenue purposes declines. In relatively rare circumstances part of the burden of a tariff may be shifted abroad especially by a country which has a buyer's monopoly or applies an export duty on a commodity of which it has a seller's monopoly. Convenience in raising revenue is an important reason for tariffs in the newer countries where sparse population makes direct taxation difficult to organise.

Tariffs are sometimes advocated as a means of fostering industries which are considered necessary or desirable. In periods of insecurity nations consider it essential to maintain various industries important for war purposes ("key" industries). They are prepared to incur the economic loss caused by the tariff as part of the cost of national preparation for war. With improvement of international relations the need for such tariffs would decline.

Certain occupations may be considered desirable for other reasons than for military power. The protection of agriculture is especially advocated as a means of ensuring the maintenance of a healthy, virile population, whether for strength in war or from the general

desire to have a healthy stock. However, with improvements in urban housing, healthier factory conditions,
the establishment of industries outside the big towns,
increased leisure-time for recreation, and transport
facilities which enable city dwellers frequently to reach
rural areas, the physical deterioration of industrial
workers and their families is likely to be much less
serious than during the nineteenth century. The working and living conditions of those employed in industry
must be raised until the factory does not involve the
breakdown of their physical qualities. To adopt a
policy, whether by a tariff or otherwise, of maintaining
a large agricultural population as a reserve which would
be drawn upon and physically deteriorated by industry
would be intolerable in a progressive community.
This argument is not in any way in conflict with the
policy of developing agriculture and of affording for
those who desire and are fitted for such work the
fullest opportunities for undertaking it.

Many countries, particularly those dependent on
mining and agriculture, have the very natural desire
for industrial development. Yet they recognise that
the free competition of the well-established industrial
countries would prevent or greatly retard their own
industrial progress. They therefore impose tariffs to
protect their "infant" industries. The reasons they
wish to develop industrially are various. The desire
for greater self-sufficiency is important; it is considered
that the prosperity of the community is too unstable
if it depends on a few products of mining or agriculture. Agricultural production may be seriously affected
periodically by adverse weather conditions, while

mineral resources are gradually exhausted. Hence industries are considered essential to the permanent welfare of the community; they also contribute to the stability of its economic life by broadening the basis of its prosperity, making it less dependent on a few products. It is argued that variety of occupations is desirable and that, for the full development of its people, a country needs skilled mechanical processes as well as agriculture and mining. Finally, it is considered that the leading industrial countries owe the strength of their position mainly to the advantage of an early start and that the newer countries would be equally efficient if they could once establish their industries.

Protection of infant industries is strongly supported and practised in various oversea countries, e.g. Australia and Canada, and is likely to become increasingly important in India and China. Also protection of infant industries is one of the reasons for high tariffs in some of the new post-war European countries. It will of course be recognised that the protection of infant industries in countries mainly dependent on natural resources imposes a burden on the mining and agricultural communities. This may be accepted for the sake of the future development of the country, but in many new countries the clash between agrarian and industrial interests is very marked, especially on the question of tariff policy.

The infant industries argument is stronger in infant industrial countries than for the protection of new industries in advanced industrial countries. One of the main advantages of tariffs for a new country is to compensate industries, which are potentially sound enough to compete on equal terms, for the handicap of remoteness from the highly developed systems of banking, distribution, and subsidiary industries of the older industrial countries.

It is evident that the infant industries argument cannot be used to support a permanent tariff. When the infant has grown to maturity, tariff protection should be gradually withdrawn. If the industry is suited to the country it will then be able to hold its own without protection. If, on the other hand, protection had been given to an industry not suited to the country, the reduction of the tariff will lead to decline of the industry. This would be an advantage as the capital and labour which would have been required for its maintenance will be diverted to more productive uses.

In practice, the withdrawal of tariffs originally imposed to protect infant industries is difficult owing to the resistance of vested interests which protection creates. Thus the infant industries argument was used legitimately during the nineteenth century to support the establishment of protective tariffs by the United States of America. Not even an American manufacturer anxious to retain tariff protection would now assert that the industries of his country are still in the stage of swaddling clothes or even in that of adolescence. America's coming of age, at least industrially, has already been celebrated; yet the tariff level is being raised rather than lowered. The United States is obsessed with the idea that high tariffs which have conduced to her industrial prosperity are essential for its continuance. Nevertheless, the United States would undoubtedly secure a balance of advantages by a

gradual reduction and even final abolition of her protective tariffs. Some of her industries would decline, but
this would be more than compensated by the gains of
the exporting industries and of consumers. The economic
gains from the abandonment of high protection would
be relatively less than those of smaller European
countries for which foreign trade is of greater importance in relation to internal trade than in the United
States.[1] Still, the economic gain to the United States
would be considerable and would be supplemented by
the political gain of improved international relations.

Tariffs are often established or advocated for the
purpose of preventing unfair foreign competition. Two
of the chief forms of such competition are dumping
and competition based on unduly low wages and other
standards of labour conditions abroad. Before tariffs
are imposed, careful investigation is necessary to
determine whether the complaint that manufacturers
are being subjected to unfair competition is justified or
not. Producers, when experiencing increasing difficulty
in marketing their output, are ready enough to raise
the cry of unfair competition though the cause of their
difficulty is an improvement in the efficiency of the
foreign manufacturer or a decline in their own. It
would evidently be unsound to grant a protective
tariff in such circumstances as it would merely put a
premium on inefficiency and withdraw the stimulus
of healthy competition. The practice of detailed
investigation into the causes of exceptionally severe

[1] The United States has the natural protection of relative isolation
from the chief industrial countries, while its size prevents heavy
or bulky imports from penetrating far into the interior owing to
high costs of transportation.

foreign competition has been adopted under the British Safeguarding of Industries Act, 1921, and a tariff is imposed only when the industry desiring protection has proved that the competition from which it is suffering is unfair.

There is no economic objection to receiving dumped goods at cheap rates if it is fairly certain that the supply will be continuous. Frequently, however, the foreign producer is merely dumping a temporary surplus or is aiming at destroying the home producer and then raising his prices. He may be enjoying a Government or other subsidy on his production or a bounty on his exports, which may at any time be withdrawn. In these circumstances the dislocation and loss to invested capital and labour in the same industry in importing countries may far outweigh the gain of the consumer. A protective tariff is therefore justified while the dumping continues. Many countries have legislation which enables tariffs to be imposed as a safeguard against dumping, but it has been found difficult in actual practice to enforce these laws.[1] More effective than tariffs would be prohibition, where deliberate State-aided dumping had been proved. This should be regarded as an emergency measure, and should be withdrawn when the conditions change.

Protection against unduly low standards of labour

---

[1] See *Memorandum on the Legislation of Different States for the Prevention of Dumping, with Special Reference to Exchange Dumping*, League of Nations document C.E.I. 7. Geneva, 1927, p. 7. This Memorandum gives a summary of the anti-dumping legislation in force in the various countries. The chief forms of dumping and their economic significance are described by Professor Viner in his *Memorandum on Dumping*, League of Nations document, C.E.C.P. 36 (1), Geneva, 1926.

conditions abroad is also difficult to establish. The question of relative labour standards in different countries is examined in some detail in a later chapter. It may, however, be noted here that frequently there is economic gain from the importation of goods produced under low labour conditions abroad. Many Western countries have derived economic benefit from the importation of goods produced under extremely low labour conditions, for example, in tropical countries. It is true that the goods have often been foodstuffs and raw materials not produced at home. Even, however, when the goods compete with home products there may be a balance of advantages, provided the foreign supply is likely to be continuous and does not by erratic variation in its competition involve sudden disorganisation of the invested capital and labour employed in the home industries. In normal times such disorganisation is less serious than in recent years as labour standards, whether in competing countries or at home, are much more stable.

The fact that labour standards are lower in one country than in another does not involve difficulty once production and trade are adjusted to these differences. Intensity of international competition, however, varies with *changes* in the levels of labour standards in different countries in relation to their efficiency. If efficiency remains unchanged, a lowering of wages or other labour standards in one country increases its competitive power, and other countries feel greater difficulty in holding their markets. But the raising or lowering of labour standards is usually gradual, and this enables capital and labour in the various countries to adapt themselves to changes in relative labour conditions.

On *economic* grounds, therefore, protection is required more against sudden and important changes than against gradual movements in relative labour standards in different countries. Action to raise labour standards in countries where working conditions are unsatisfactory is, of course, desirable on humanitarian grounds, but protective tariffs are obviously useless for this purpose.

The chief difficulties in imposing countervailing duties on goods produced by labour abroad working longer hours and for lower wages than labour at home are (1) the determination as to whether competition is unfair, and if so, to what extent; (2) the necessity of imposing differential rates of duty on goods from each country; (3) the establishment of a system of certificates of origin. To determine whether the competition is unfair it is not enough merely to show that hourly or weekly wages are lower and hours of labour longer than those in the home industry. Frequently low labour standards and low efficiency of production are found together. To determine, therefore, whether competition is unfair it is necessary to consider not only labour standards but also labour costs per unit of output. At present the data available on labour costs in different countries are very meagre and quite inadequate for the purpose of determining whether competition is fair or not.

Tariffs giving preference to the products of certain countries are often supported more on political than on economic grounds. Preferential tariffs granted for political reasons are especially dangerous to good international relations because of the hostility they arouse in countries against which differentiation is practised. The policy of preferences is examined with special reference to British Empire trade policy in the following section.

Tariffs for bargaining have been found in practice to increase rather than reduce barriers to international trade. On the other hand, free trade and low tariff countries have usually enjoyed, through the operation of the most-favoured-nation clause, the advantages which other countries have secured by bargaining. Retaliatory tariffs, no doubt, give psychological satisfaction because of the injury they inflict on the foreigner, though they cannot contribute to economic welfare at home.

D

CHAPTER III

THE BRITISH TARIFF SITUATION

The prolonged post-war depression and especially its severity in 1930 with over two million workers unemployed has induced increasing numbers of people to doubt the present value of British traditional free trade policy. There is a growing belief that the old policy is not suited to the new conditions of industry and trade. All attempts to conquer unemployment have failed, and in desperation the electorate seems ready to endorse any programme which offers a new method of attack. Consequently the political possibility of a fundamental change in British tariff policy is now stronger than at any time during at least a generation. It is therefore of interest to review the present position of British industry and to consider how far a change in policy would be likely to contribute to the welfare of the British people. Also, the British position is fairly representative of other free trade and low tariff countries.

Most British supporters of protection will admit readily enough that free trade would be a sound policy if practised also by other countries. But they point to failure of the efforts made by successive British Governments to secure reductions of foreign tariffs and doubt whether any substantial reductions are likely to be effected in the early future. They claim that British industry is both injured by foreign tariffs and handicapped by absence of British tariffs. They therefore consider that a change of policy is essential for the restoration of prosperity.

Before examining the various proposals which are being made, a brief review is necessary of the position of British industry and trade, with special reference to the importance of imports and exports. Of all nations Britain is the most dependent on international trade, and is more seriously injured than any other by factors which cause its reduction.[1] The main features of British foreign trade in 1913, 1928, and 1929 are tabulated on page 52. The statistics show the outstanding importance of imports of food, drink, tobacco, and raw materials from foreign countries and also from British countries including both the Colonies and self-governing countries of the British Commonwealth. They also show the large total value of manufactured goods exported; in 1929 the value exported to foreign countries was about 53 per cent. and that to British countries about 47 per cent. of total exports of manufactured goods. To these figures of visible exports should be added the large value of invisible exports, especially shipping and financial services.[2] The table also shows the high value of manufactured goods imported into Britain from foreign countries; some, but certainly not all, of these imports do not compete with British products.

Statistics showing the value of British exports to various countries in 1913, 1928, and 1929 are given in the table on page 53 :

[1] A detailed account of the factors affecting British trade is given by the Committee on Industry and Trade in its *Survey of Overseas Markets*, London 1925, and in its *Final Report*, London 1929 (Cmd. 3282).

[2] These more than outweigh the adverse balance of visible imports over visible exports; the excess is invested overseas, but the amount available for this purpose is now considerably less than before the war.

VALUE OF IMPORTS AND EXPORTS OF THE UNITED KINGDOM IN 1913, 1928, AND 1929[1]

(In Millions of Pounds Sterling)

Articles and Group of Countries	Imports			Exports[2]		
	1913	1928	1929	1913	1928	1929
Food, drink, and tobacco						
Foreign countries	214·2	330·0	345·6	19·8	22·7	23·1
British countries	76·0	200·9	189·9	12·8	31·6	32·6
Raw materials and articles mainly unmanufactured						
Foreign countries	190·3	213·1	212·3	66·0	62·1	69·8
British countries	91·5	121·5	127·3	3·9	8·1	9·1
Articles wholly or mainly manufactured						
Foreign countries	170·2	283·3	299·3	237·5	303·2	303·9
British countries	23·3	34·5	35·1	173·8	275·6	269·9
TOTAL (including other classes of imports and exports)						
Foreign countries	577·2	832·0	861·9	329·9	395·9	404·9
British countries	191·5	363·6	358·9	195·3	327·7	324·4

[1] *Statistical Abstract for the United Kingdom.* The 1928 and 1929 figures are not strictly comparable with those for 1913 owing to the adoption of a new classification and because they include trade with the Irish Free State. The figures make no allowance for the difference between the value of money between 1913 and recent years.

[2] Exports of United Kingdom produce, not including imports which were re-exported within the year.

VALUE OF BRITISH EXPORTS TO VARIOUS COUNTRIES IN 1913, 1928, AND 1929 [1]

(In Millions of Pounds Sterling)

Country	1913	1928 [5]	1929 [5]
British countries			
Canada	23·8	34·5	35·0
Australia	34·5	55·7	54·2
South Africa	22·2	31·5	32·5
British India	70·3	83·9	78·2
Irish Free State	—	35·1	36·1
New Zealand	10·8	19·3	21·4
Other British countries [2]	33·7	67·7	67·0
TOTAL, British countries	195·3	327·7	324·4
Foreign countries			
European			
France	28·9	25·2	31·7
Germany	40·7	40·9	37·0
Scandinavian countries	20·2	27·4	31·1
Netherlands	15·4	21·8	21·8
Belgium	13·2	17·0	19·4
Italy	14·6	14·4	16·0
Russia	18·1	2·7 [6]	3·7 [6]
Switzerland	4·2	7·9	6·4
Spain	7·9	9·8	12·1
Other European countries [3]	13·0	31·6	29·9
Extra-European			
United States of America	29·3	46·7	45·6
Argentine	22·6	31·2	29·1
China	14·8	15·7	14·0
Japan	14·5	14·5	13·4
Brazil	12·5	16·0	13·4
Egypt	9·8 [4]	11·2	12·6
Other Extra-European	50·2	61·9	67·7
TOTAL, foreign countries	329·9	395·9	404·9
TOTAL, all countries	525·2	723·6	729·3

[1] *Statistical Abstract for the United Kingdom.* The figures do not include the value of re-exports.   [2] Mainly colonies.
[3] Excluding Turkey.   [4] Including Anglo-Egyptian Sudan.
[5] The 1928 and 1929 figures are for post-war areas.
[6] This fall is partly because of the constitution of new States (Finland, Esthonia, Latvia, Lithuania, and Poland).

During the nineteenth century Britain had a considerable start before other countries in most manufacturing industries. Markets for her goods were easy to find, competition was not intense, and manufactures were largely exchanged for food or raw materials. This happy condition was passing away even before the war, other nations were becoming increasingly industrialised and competition was growing more severe. The World War and the high foreign tariffs of post-war years accelerated the change. Many European countries have approached nearer to Britain's industrial level; the United States has "come of age", while Japan especially, but also India, China, and the self-governing countries of the British Commonwealth are developing their manufacturing industries. Britain's industrial position is therefore seriously menaced and competition greatly intensified.

Industrial developments abroad were inevitable, but in normal circumstances would have been much more gradual. This would have enabled Britain to adapt her industrial structure systematically to the new conditions. Actually very marked changes have been concentrated in a few years. No adaptation was possible during the war years when the only consideration was the use of industry for war purposes. This seriously aggravated Britain's subsequent difficulties by involving the over-development of certain industries, particularly coal-mining, in which the investment of capital and labour would otherwise have tended to diminish. Also the world economic chaos of the early post-war years hindered the progress of adjustment. Only during the last few years have the needs of the situation been realised.

British industries which were developed to supply a world market must evidently decline in size as other countries establish their own factories. The cotton textile industry is perhaps the chief example. Cotton weaving is usually one of the first industries to be set up in a country which has industrial aspirations.[1] Comparatively little capital is required; weaving can be operated on a small scale and the skill required to weave ordinary qualities is easily acquired. At first yarns are imported and spinning develops later. The marked progress made, especially by Oriental countries, has seriously undermined Lancashire's prosperity. This is reflected in British exports of cotton yarns and cloths. The money value of exports of unbleached yarn was over £18·5 millions in 1929 compared with £12·7 millions in 1913, but the money value of exports of unbleached grey piece goods had fallen from £27·4 millions in 1913 to £19·6 millions in 1929.[2]

The cotton industry has, however, experienced little competition from foreign imports into Britain. The coal-mining industry is completely free from foreign competition in the home market although the over-development of the industry both in Britain and abroad has greatly intensified competition in foreign markets. Certain other important industries have, however, experienced the competition of foreign manufactured goods in Britain. Thus in the iron and steel industry the money value of imports of bars,

[1] This development is reviewed, both for cotton and wool, by Professor E. B. Dietrich, of Mount Holyoke College, Massachusetts, in articles published in the *International Labour Review*, October and November 1930.
[2] In 1930 the figures were: unbleached yarn, £13 millions, and unbleached piece goods, £10 millions.

rods, angles, shapes, and sections rose from £4·6 millions in 1913 to £7·4 millions in 1930. In other branches of the iron and steel industry also imports grew considerably. On the other hand, while there was a marked fall in the value of pig-iron and ferro-alloys exported there was a considerable rise in exports of tubes, pipes, and fittings. In certain branches of the woollen industry, especially the manufacture of carpets and rugs, British industry has lost ground.

A consequence of the increasing competition of foreign manufactures in the home market has been increase in the demand for protective tariffs. This has been particularly marked in the iron and steel industry, but has also been considerable in the woollen and in certain other industries.

The main lines of the changes in imports and exports are indicated by the statistics tabulated opposite for several important groups of manufactured articles. The figures show the growth in the money value of foreign manufactures imported into Britain. They indicate the large balance of exports which still prevails in most branches; the economic basis of Lancashire's "liberalism" is specially evident. This balance of exports is significant in any decision on tariff policy.

To summarise, Britain has lost ground industrially during recent years in relation to other countries. Many changes have been concentrated in a short period instead of being spread over a generation or more. This has involved loss of capital and employment in the industries which had developed on a scale to supply large world markets no longer available. A more gradual evolution would have enabled loss of

VALUE OF IMPORTS AND EXPORTS OF VARIOUS MANUFACTURED ARTICLES BY THE UNITED KINGDOM IN 1913, 1929, AND 1930 [1]

(In Millions of Pounds Sterling)

Articles	Imports			Exports		
	1913	1929	1930	1913	1929	1930
Iron and steel	15·9	24·7	23·3	55·3	68·0	51·3
Machinery and parts thereof	7·3	19·2	17·9	33·6	54·4	46·9
Cotton yarns, cloth, etc.	9·2	10·9	9·7	126·5	135·4	87·6
Woollen and worsted yarns, cloth, etc.[5]	9·6	15·2	13·3	30·2	45·6	33·1
Clothing[3]	11·1	18·9	18·2	18·5	21·6	17·4
Chemicals, drugs, dyes, colours	13·3	16·9	13·6	19·5	26·6	22·0
Leather[4]	10·6	14·4	13·7	3·5	6·2	4·0
Paper and cardboard	7·7	18·0	18·0	3·7	9·8	8·5
Vehicles (rail)	—	0·1	0·1	6·1	10·1	10·0
Vehicles (road)[5]	8·0	10·2	6·4	7·6	22·0	18·3
Ships and boats (new)	—	0·2	0·2	11·0	15·5	19·9

[1] Compiled from *Statistical Abstract for the United Kingdom* and supplementary data supplied by the Board of Trade. The figures make no allowance for changes in the value of money between 1913 and recent years.

[2] Includes carpets and rugs.

[3] Includes garments, boots and shoes, gloves, hats, and hosiery.

[4] Undressed and dressed.

[5] Includes rubber tyres and tubes.

capital to be avoided and unemployment to have been relatively small. Worn-out capital equipment would not have been replaced in over-developed industries and other industries more suited to the changing conditions would have expanded.

British difficulties are due not only to foreign tariffs and the growth of industries under their protection, but also to the relative advance in efficiency made by several competing countries, especially in Europe. For some years Germany, Sweden, Czechoslovakia and other continental countries have energetically rationalised their industries. In reconstructing the devastated areas of Northern France modern plant was installed, while Belgian industry has also been re-equipped by the aid of reparations.[1] It should not be implied that British industry is making no efforts to keep up to date. Especially since 1927 the need for rationalisation has been increasingly recognised. Previously many British manufacturers had looked for a recovery of markets merely by the restoration of world economic prosperity and by cessation of inflation abroad.

In addition to gaining relatively in the efficiency of their equipment, Continental competitors have had advantages in relative wage levels. Owing to the retarding effect of customary standards of living, wages in many European countries seem to have risen more slowly than the productive efficiency of industry; consequently they have contributed to low

[1] The position of the Continental iron and steel industry is well indicated in the Economic Advisory Council's *Report of Delegation on the Industrial Conditions in the Iron and Steel Industries in France, Belgium, Luxemburg, Germany, and Czechoslovakia*, London 1930, Cmd. 3601.

costs of production per unit of output. The wage relation was also disturbed by the low levels reached during currency depreciation in Germany, France, and other countries, and the slowness with which the normal levels have been restored. The French method of stabilising the franc while internal prices were below the world level also contributed to low labour costs; however, the disputes in the textile and metal industries in Northern France in the summer of 1930 reveal growing pressure by the workers to secure wage increases. On the other hand, wage rates in Britain are relatively high, having lacked elasticity in adjustment to falling prices. This is true more of the sheltered industries than of those exposed to foreign competition, but the general effect has been high labour costs of production.

In the circumstances two courses are open to Britain: first, to pursue a policy for becoming steadily more self-sufficient; second, systematically to direct British capital and labour into those industries where they will have the greatest efficiency relative to industry abroad and will contribute most to the maintenance or expansion of the export trade. The first aim may be summarily dismissed. Britain is too dependent on foreign trade to justify any attempt at self-sufficiency; British resources, not supplemented largely by foreign trade, are inadequate to maintain the present population at the present standard of living. Greater self-sufficiency achieved by high tariffs would tend seriously to increase unemployment, especially as mass emigration of surplus population is no longer possible.[1]

[1] The Balfour Committee considered self-sufficiency to be impossible apart from mass emigration.

The second course demands a considerable and rapid adjustment of the balance between British manufactures to post-war conditions of world industry and commerce. The problem is almost entirely one of efficiency and initiative. To fall behind in efficiency would inevitably involve a decline in British standards of living relative to those abroad. Britain's industrial future seems to lie in reducing costs of the goods now exported, in the development of the finer qualities of goods, and in keeping a leading place in new industries. Young industrial countries often begin by producing low and medium qualities in the old industries; this is true, for example, of cotton textiles manufactured in Eastern Europe and in Asiatic countries. As the world's wealth and standard of consumption increase there will be a growing demand for the finer qualities of the necessaries of life and for a wide variety of miscellaneous products, either conventional necessaries or semi-luxuries. It is essential that on the basis of a systematic study of the trends of world demand and sources of supply the older British industries should be adapted to the changed conditions and the development of the newer industries encouraged. The problem to be considered here is the extent to which tariffs can accelerate this transition.

Three chief tariff measures are being advocated:

(1) A low general tariff on all manufactured goods or on food and manufactured goods; 10 per cent. is the rate most discussed.

(2) A system of preferences within the British Commonwealth; this is often related to the first proposal.

(3) Safeguarding.

A Low General Tariff

A low general tariff on manufactured goods only is mainly supported as a source of revenue, and as a means of reducing unemployment by affording some protection to British manufactures. For an election programme it has the advantage of being clear and simple. Many people, ready to accept almost any device as a way out of the present difficulty, are persuaded that a 10 per cent. tariff could not do much harm and might do some good. They are of opinion that it would provide a psychological stimulus to British industrialists. They assert that the maintenance of free trade in Britain in the hope that other countries will be induced to come into line is impracticable and quixotic. They claim that by adopting a 10 per cent. tariff on manufactures Britain would merely bring herself into line with the low tariff countries and could still work internationally for the general establishment of low tariffs throughout the world.

Discussion of such a tariff primarily for revenue is somewhat outside the scope of the present volume. It would involve a review of the relation, in the British system of taxation, between the burden of direct and indirect taxes on different classes of the community.

A general tariff would enable British producers of manufactured goods for the home market to raise their prices. This would increase their prosperity and their scale of production would expand, despite some decline in demand due to higher prices. But among these industries would be some in which Britain's efficiency

NUMBERS AND PERCENTAGES OF INSURED PERSONS RECORDED AS UNEMPLOYED IN GREAT BRITAIN AND NORTHERN IRELAND AT JULY 22, 1929, JULY 21, 1930, AND JANUARY 26, 1931[1]

Industry	July 22, 1929		July 21, 1930		January 26, 1931	
	Numbers Unemployed	Percentages	Numbers Unemployed	Percentages	Numbers Unemployed	Percentages
Coal mining	203,002	18·2	302,620	28·2	208,821	19·5
Other mining[2]	12,527	8·4	24,620	15·8	38,115	24·4
Brick, pottery, glass, etc.	22,440	11·5	39,207	19·5	55,396	26·5
Chemicals	12,837	5·9	22,929	10·5	31,650	14·5
Steel melting, iron and steel rolling	35,591	19·9	58,996	33·0	81,760	45·2
Other metal manufacture	16,502	11·5	30,852	21·2	49,627	34·0
Engineering	63,748	8·5	120,359	15·9	187,752	24·4
Construction and repair of vehicles	24,175	7·8	49,252	15·4	53,974	16·9
Shipbuilding and repairing	46,965	23·2	64,895	31·7	95,329	46·6
Metal trades	41,307	8·1	87,927	16·6	117,223	21·1
Cotton textiles	80,165	14·5	251,884	45·4	247,517[4]	43·9
Woollen and worsted textiles	37,767	15·6	62,858	26·3	75,335	31·3
Other textiles	56,407	10·9	141,737	27·2	172,419	32·3

Leather and leather goods	5,884	8·7	9,331	13·8	13,182	19·9
Tailoring	12,725	6·4	23,687	11·9	41,149	20·4
Boots and shoes, etc.	18,893	14·0	24,576	18·2	28,905	21·3
Other clothing trades	10,613	4·3	20,077	8·1	35,563	14·3
Food, drink, and tobacco	33,708	6·6	53,185	10·4	77,272	14·7
Saw-milling, furniture, etc. ..	14,932	7·2	26,734	12·4	43,644	20·0
Printing and paper trades ..	14,633	3·9	27,023	6·9	42,580	10·7
Building and construction ..	102,804	10·5	160,727	16·2	288,052	28·3
Other manufacturing industries .	9,175	6·1	19,184	12·2	30,467	19·2
Gas, water, and electricity supply ..	8,777	5·4	11,966	7·4	15,049	9·1
Transport and communication ..	104,573	13·3	139,043	17·2	188,451	23·0
Distributive trades	91,149	5·6	146,138	8·7	213,157	12·1
Commerce, banking, etc.	5,615	2·5	8,146	3·6	11,690	5·0
Miscellaneous trades and services[3] ..	90,593	7·8	142,135	11·7	218,763	17·1
TOTAL	1,177,507	9·9	2,070,088	17·1	2,662,842	21·5

[1] Compiled from *The Ministry of Labour Gazette*, August 1929, August 1930, and February 1931.

[2] Including non-metalliferous mining products.

[3] Including national and local government services, hotels and boarding houses, and fishing.

[4] Excluding persons disqualified for benefit by the trade dispute.

is relatively small. It would seem preferable, if protection is to be accorded, to reserve it for the most promising branches of industry and not give it indiscriminately to all. This would, however, involve the difficulty of selection and would open the door for pressure by the various interests.

A general tariff on manufactured goods while benefiting the producer of these goods for the home market would injure all other British producers of goods and services for the home market by raising costs. Also, demand for these goods and services would decline because the increased cost of protected manufactures would cause reduction of purchasing power available to satisfy other needs. Production for exports would also incur higher costs. A general tariff cannot, therefore, be seriously proposed as a remedy for unemployment in view of the large numbers unemployed in industries and services which would suffer rather than benefit from the tariff. This is illustrated by the statistics of unemployment tabulated on pages 62 and 63. Figures are given for July 1929 before the world depression of trade, for July 1930 when unemployment had almost doubled, and for January 1931 when the two and a half million mark had been passed.

Of the numbers unemployed in July 1930 and January 1931, one-half were in industries and services not suffering from foreign competition in the home market. Chief among these industries and services were building and public works contracting, ship-building and ship-repairing, transport and communication, the distributive trades, national and local government, entertainments and sports, hotel boarding and club

services, gas, water, and electricity supply. Over
200,000 were in coal-mining; there is no import
of foreign coal into Britain. In cotton textiles, with
about 250,000 unemployed in January 1931, imports
are negligible in comparison with the export trade.
Many branches of other industries encounter little
foreign competition in the home market or are pre-
dominantly exporting. It is probable, therefore, that
during recent years about three-quarters of the unemployed have been in industries which would suffer injury
from a general tariff on manufactures. So precarious is
the position of the export industries that serious harm
might be done by even the slight increase in costs
which would result from a low tariff of 10 per cent.
on manufactured imports. Such a tariff would not
solve the unemployment problem and would tend to
aggravate the situation in those industries where
depression is the most severe.

A tariff on food-stuffs as well as on manufactured
goods would be still more serious in its effects on
British industry. The rise in the cost of living would
be greater than that due to a tariff only on manufactured imports. British agriculture would benefit,
but in determining the balance of advantages the
greater importance of industry relatively to agriculture
is decisive.

It is argued that since British real wage rates are
unduly high in consequence of the more rapid fall in
recent years of wholesale prices and the cost of living
than of money wages, the rise in the cost of living
resulting from the tariff would benefit British industry
by reducing real wages. But this gain would be counter-

balanced by loss of purchasing power of home consumers; this would reduce the consumption of goods and services of industries and occupations which could not use the tariff as a means for raising their prices.

Tariffs on foreign food-stuffs are usually included in programmes for British Empire Preference.[1] They are considered in this connection in the following section.

BRITISH EMPIRE PREFERENCE

The general arguments in support of British Empire Preference, or, as it should perhaps be styled, British Commonwealth Preference, are partly political and partly economic. The economic arguments are often based on the view that although Britain is too small and lacks too many of the products necessary for self-sufficiency, the area and products of the Empire are adequate for this purpose. The chief proposals are (1) Empire Free Trade, with import duties on foreign products; (2) a tariff on foreign food-stuffs and manufactured articles and lower rates on Empire products.

The proposal for Empire Free Trade does not demand lengthy discussion. It might be of advantage to British manufacturing industries, but is impracticable owing to the opposition of the self-governing Dominions and India. These are determined to develop industrially and to increase their own self-sufficiency. They therefore fear British manufactures as much as

[1] For convenience and in conformity with what is still common practice the expression "British Empire" is used, unless otherwise indicated, to cover the self-governing countries of the British Commonwealth of Nations together with British colonies and dependencies.

those from foreign countries. It is true that the self-governing countries of the British Commonwealth of Nations grant valuable preferences to British manu-factures. But they still impose high tariffs on British imports as a protection for their own infant industries. The Balfour Committee on Industry and Trade in its *Survey of Overseas Markets* calls attention (page 15) to "the remarkable fact that the main increases of tariff rates on British exports have been within the British Empire . . . ".

In imposing these higher tariffs the Dominions are acting in the interest of their own industrial develop-ment. The Canadian Conservative Government's policy has been expressed in the phrase "Canada first, the Empire second." This principle is adopted by all overseas Dominions, and, as they are anxious to pro-tect and develop their industries, proposals for Empire Free Trade are utterly futile.[1] This was emphasised by representatives of the Dominions at the Imperial Conference, 1930.

The proposal for a British tariff on foreign food-stuffs, raw materials and manufactures, with lower rates on, or even free entry of, Empire products, is at least practicable. It depends on British action only and not on an attempt to reconcile the widely divergent economic policies of a number of self-governing units.

In deciding about the value of such preference the effects on British industry and trade are the primary considerations. A general tariff on manufactured goods

[1] Empire Free Trade in the narrower sense to cover only Great Britain and the colonial areas would be more practicable. It would, however, be injurious to British manufacturing industries if foreign supplies of food and raw materials were taxed.

only with preferential rates on those manufactured in the British Empire is open to the same objections as those raised in the previous section against a general tariff on manufactured imports. Its modification by granting preferential rates on goods manufactured within the British Empire is of little significance; imports of manufactured goods from Empire countries represent little more than 10 per cent. of total British imports of these goods.

To have any considerable value, Empire preferences must include tariffs on foreign food-stuffs or raw materials or both with lower rates on imports of these products from Empire countries. Such tariffs on raw materials are rarely proposed because they would so clearly hamper British industry and trade by increasing costs. British industry is dependent on foreign countries for nearly two-thirds of its raw materials.

A tax on foreign food-stuffs with preferential rates or freedom from duties on imports from Empire countries would be of considerable value to those countries. It would also be of some assistance to British agriculture. But it is necessary to remember that foreign countries supply Britain with more than 60 per cent. of her requirements of food, drink, and tobacco. A tax on foreign imports which would give preferences of any value to Empire products and protection to British agriculture would seriously raise the British cost of living. It would also lead to a reduction of exports of British manufactures to foreign countries.[1]

[1] The Balfour Committee in their *Final Report* (page 24) discussed the value of the granting by Britain of preferences to Empire products. They stated that to do so "would involve the imposition

While the British system is mainly free trade, with only a few small preferences, foreign countries are willing to accord most-favoured-nation treatment. There would be little hope of this being continued if Britain granted large preferences to the Dominions; and tariff discriminations by foreign countries against British trade would be far more serious than high tariffs. Whereas high tariffs reduce world trade, discrimination would reduce the British share of world trade.

It may be concluded, therefore, that Empire Free Trade is impracticable and that a system of British tariffs with preferential rates on Empire products would be harmful to British industry. In attempting to maintain and develop British trade a restriction mainly to the Empire would inevitably be injurious. Maximum freedom should be retained to take advantage of any favourable opportunity for trade whether in the Empire or elsewhere.

This conclusion does not imply any lack of sympathy with plans for promoting Empire economic cooperation, but merely excludes tariffs as a suitable method. The extensive trade between Britain and the Empire has been built up without important British preferential tariffs. It can be continued and extended by other means than that of tariffs. Advantages are accorded

of duties on staple food-stuffs and raw materials to the serious detriment of our exporting power, in order to give a preference thereon to Empire products. We are convinced that no Dominion would *mutatis mutandis* be willing to adopt a similar policy, and we do not believe that they would expect or wish Great Britain to do so. We believe that the necessary basis of all sound commercial relations among the States of the British Empire is the full and general recognition of the principle that prior regard is due to the essential needs and interests of the home population."

to Empire countries in their financial operations, especially loans. A large part of the cost of Imperial defence is borne by Britain. The activities of the Empire Marketing Board contribute to the increase of trade in Empire products, while a permanent Imperial Economic Organisation could effect valuable coordination of policy. This must be based on mutual recognition of Britain's need for food and raw materials at low price and the desire of the Dominions for industrial development even at the cost of loss to the Mother Country.

SAFEGUARDING

If Britain should decide to impose tariffs to protect its manufacturing industries it would be preferable to do so by somewhat modifying and extending the principle of safeguarding than by a general tariff on all manufactured goods imported. A general tariff has the advantage of simplicity, but it would apply indiscriminately both to manufactures which compete with British products and to those which do not. It would also protect branches of industry for which Britain is not well suited.

Procedure under the Safeguarding of Industries Act is more complicated, involving detailed investigations before protection is granted. But it has the advantage that protection can be accorded to industries which are most likely to benefit; also the amount of protection can be adapted to the circumstances of each industry. If, as is sometimes proposed, the system of special investigations were abolished, there would be no practical difference between safeguarding and ordinary protection.

At present few industries are protected by safeguarding duties, and out of every two hundred British workers only about one is employed in these industries.[1] Before a duty can be accorded, an industry desiring protection must make application for the imposition of an import duty and must satisfy a committee of enquiry appointed by the Board of Trade that:

(1) the applicant industry is of substantial importance;

(2) abnormal quantities of the class of goods produced are being imported;

(3) the prices of the imported goods are lower than those at which similar goods can be profitably manufactured at home;

(4) competition of the imports causes or is likely to cause serious unemployment in the British industry;

(5) the exceptional competition is due to subsidies, bounties, or other artificial advantages, or to inferior labour conditions (wages, hours, etc.);

(6) the applicant industry is being carried on with reasonable efficiency and economy;

(7) the imposition of a duty would not cause serious unemployment in industries using the goods in production.[2]

[1] The goods liable to safeguarding and other protective duties (chiefly the McKenna duties) only amount to 2 or 3 per cent. of British imports. (Statement submitted by the British Members to the International Economic Conference, League of Nations document C.E.I. 29, 1st Series, page 25.)

[2] These conditions are given in the White Paper on *Safeguarding of Industries—Procedure and Enquiries*, Cmd. 2327, London, 1925.

It is not denied that some economic advantage might be derived from a judicious application of the principle of safeguarding during the next few years. Reference has already been made to the special difficulties with which British industry is faced from the concentration of vital changes in world industry and trade within an exceptionally short period. Normally these changes would have been more gradual and British industry would have adapted itself readily to the new conditions.

Two kinds of industry might benefit from temporary safeguarding. First are branches of industries producing mainly for the home market which have fallen behind in efficiency and are in need of rationalisation. They are at present in a relatively defenceless condition, like the crab when changing its shell. Such sick industries, equally with infant industries, might benefit from temporary protection. Healthy efficient industries need no protection; the cry for protection is raised only by sick industries and somewhat resembles the same mentality as the cry for the dole, but with less justification.

Similarly, protection might assist the progress of industries which are at present in an early stage of development but which are likely to be prominent in the future. Britain's industrial supremacy in the nineteenth century was due largely to being first in the field, with her industries developed to maturity while other countries were lagging far behind. It is not to be expected that Britain can secure the same lead in the twentieth century, but there might be advantages in hastening to maturity the industries of the future. On these lines protection has been afforded to certain industries, especially artificial silk and motor-cars; aerial transportation is fostered by other methods. The need for the protection of these new industries often implies that Britain has been slower than other countries in developing them and that foreign imports into Britain are hampering the progress of the British industry.

The practical application of the principle of safeguarding for these purposes would involve difficulties. One of the chief would be the selection of the industries to be protected, and this would be attended by the clamour of vested interests. Selection would demand detailed Government investigations. It would be necessary to avoid protecting industries in which foreign countries are likely to show superior efficiency; such industries would inevitably decline when protection was withdrawn. The task would be especially difficult of determining in which among the developing industries Britain is likely to show high efficiency in relation to foreign producers. Difficulties would also arise in deciding the duration of protection and the methods of its withdrawal.

In addition to these practical difficulties protection would result in higher prices to consumers. A policy of safeguarding would not cure unemployment. This can only be reduced on a large scale by general progress in industrial efficiency, reasonable adjustment of wage and other costs, and the securing of greater international liberty of trading. The granting of protection to a considerable number of industries would also weaken the moral force of Britain's leadership in advocating reduction of tariffs by international agreement.

Consequently the balance of advantages seems to be against an extension of safeguarding.[1]

This somewhat detailed survey of the British position has been given because of its own interest and because of the importance of British policy on the future trend of world tariffs. The conclusion has been reached that a general tariff on manufactured goods would be of economic disadvantage to the British people, as would Empire Preference on an extensive scale, while Empire Free Trade has been judged to be impracticable. The economic advantages of judicious safeguarding have been indicated, as have also its difficulties and dangers. Against the economic advantages, however, has been set the loss of influence by Britain in international action for greater freedom of trade. While this issue is in the balance it would be a tragedy if the raising of British tariffs, whether safeguarding or other, were a deciding factor in confirming other countries in the creed of economic nationalism.

Reference will be made later to indications that a movement for lower tariffs may achieve success during the next decade. The Balfour Committee which supported the maintenance, with minor exceptions, of British free trade policy stated that: "Generally speak-

---

[1] For a few industries subsidies might be granted to encourage their development. Subsidies would be better adapted than tariffs for hastening the growth of young industries not yet exposed to serious foreign competition. In this connection it is interesting to quote from Sir William Beveridge's book on *Unemployment: a Problem of Industry*, London, 1930. He says, "Selective subsidies to decaying industries, or, rather, for the employment of men displaced from such industries may have economic advantages as definitely as may protection of infant industries".

ing, we are of opinion that Great Britain's major interest is to take a leading part in negotiating and participating in international conventions, if only for the purpose of influencing other countries in the direction of gradual conformity to the basic liberal principles underlying British commercial and economic policy."[1] This influence would be reduced, and other countries would tend to maintain their policy if at this stage Britain were to adopt a programme of increasing her tariffs.

If, however, it should become evident after repeated efforts to secure greater liberty of trading abroad that economic nationalism is permanently entrenched behind high tariff barriers, Britain will be likely to abandon her free trade policy, aim at greater self-sufficiency, face a relative decline in standard of living, and would be justified in preparing for the next war.

[1] *Final Report*, p. 21.

CHAPTER IV

MEASURES FOR SECURING GREATER LIBERTY OF INTERNATIONAL TRADE

The present chapter deals with abolition of import and export prohibitions and reduction of tariffs. Reference is made to the measures attempted or contemplated by the League of Nations. The removal of other barriers to international trade and the highly technical problems often involved are not discussed.[1]

REMOVAL OF PROHIBITIONS

The most formidable barrier to international trade is absolute prohibition. For a considerable number of commodities import or export prohibitions were introduced by many countries during the war and in the early post-war years. Some of these prohibitions were gradually withdrawn by decisions of individual States, but progress was so slow that a diplomatic conference for the abolition of import and export prohibitions and restrictions was convened by the

---

[1] They include direct and indirect subsidies, export duties, transport and other discriminations. Among other questions not discussed are simplification of customs tariffs, unification of tariff nomenclature, simplification of Customs formalities, and the obligation to affix a mark of origin on goods. These various subjects are reviewed in documents submitted to the World Economic Conference, especially in C.E.I. 5 (1), 20, 32, 33, and 42, in C.E.C.P. 96, and in the *Final Report* of the Conference, C.E.I. 44 (1). Action subsequently taken by the League of Nations and by various countries is described in reports of the Economic Consultative Committee on *Application of the Recommendations of the International Economic Conference.*

League of Nations and held in Geneva during October
and November 1927. The Conference, which was
attended by delegates from thirty-five States, adopted
an International Convention for the abolition of existing
prohibitions or restrictions and the non-imposition of
new ones.[1] The Convention permits various exceptions
of a non-economic character, for example, the protection of public health or the protection of animals
and plants against disease, and prohibitions or restrictions imposed on moral or humanitarian grounds.
States were also allowed to make other specified
exceptions; thus the British Government retained the
right temporarily to prohibit the import of certain
dye-stuffs. The Convention would, however, when
ratified, free almost all natural products and manufactured articles from prohibitions and from the chief
restrictions other than tariffs.

The Convention was signed by about thirty States,
but difficulty was experienced in securing sufficient
ratifications and the Convention has not been fully
applied. Seven countries, including Great Britain and
the United States, ratified unconditionally and are at
present bound by the Convention, although they are
free to claim release after July 1, 1931. Many countries,
however, made their ratification conditional upon the
accession of other States. All the necessary ratifications were secured except that of Poland, whose

[1] The text of the Convention and the proceedings of the Conference
are given in League of Nations document C. 21. M. 12. 1928. II.
See also C.E.I. 22. Already several years earlier a Convention on
Simplification of Customs Formalities and several Conventions to
secure greater freedom of transit had been adopted in conferences
called together by the League of Nations.

abstention has rendered the Convention largely ineffective. An attempt will, no doubt, be made to overcome the difficulty, but the fate of this Convention
indicates the roughness of the road to greater liberty
of trading.

Even before the Conference for the abolition of
prohibitions the problem of tariffs had been given
chief attention by the World Economic Conference,
Geneva, May 1927. The object of the Conference was to
focus public opinion on obstacles to world economic
progress and to secure agreement on principles and
methods for their diminution or removal. Two of the
chief conclusions were: (1) that tariffs, though within
the sovereign jurisdiction of the separate States, are
not a matter of purely domestic interest but greatly
influence the trade of the world; (2) that the time has
come to put an end to the increase in tariffs and move
in the opposite direction.[1] These and other recommendations received enthusiastic approval by the
Conference and by the Assembly of the League of
Nations. But they involved no obligation on the various
States to take action, and the sequel has been con-
tinuously disappointing. It is true that a sharp upward
movement was arrested and that tariffs would undoubtedly have been considerably higher but for
the restraining influence of the Conference. No fundamental change in policy has, however, been made
and there has been no general movement of tariff
reduction.

[1] *Final Report*, p. 30.

TARIFF REDUCTIONS

There are three methods by which tariffs may be reduced, and all were recommended by the World Economic Conference. They are: (1) unilateral action, i.e. a change by an individual State without corresponding measures by any other State; (2) bilateral commercial treaties; (3) collective or multilateral agreements.

By unilateral action a number of countries which in 1927 were preparing new tariffs at levels much above those previously in force considerably moderated their proposals under the influence of the World Economic Conference; the new tariffs were, however, somewhat above the old levels. Subsequently, unilateral action for tariff reduction has had negligible results, while several countries have raised the levels of their Customs duties. Nor are important reductions by unilateral action likely to be made in the early future. It is difficult to secure the necessary support of public opinion for reduction in any country unless there is a reasonable prospect of downward movements in other countries. Vested interests point to high tariffs abroad and are quick to exploit the argument that reductions should be made only by reciprocity.

There is stronger support for changes by agreement with other countries; many people who oppose unilateral action are ready to admit the advantages of mutual reductions through bilateral treaties or collective agreements. Important bilateral treaties were concluded in 1927 and many reductions made. Unfortunately further progress by this method has since been meagre and its prospects are doubtful. Similarly, attempts to secure collective agreements have to the present given disappointing results. This has been due in part to inadequate support by public opinion. Sir Arthur Salter has emphasised in his Memorandum on *The "United States of Europe" Idea* that trade barriers are buttressed by some private interest which has developed business under their protection. "These interests are better organised, more vocal, and more politically effective than the general public interests on the other side; and are much more conscious of what they would stand to lose than the other business interests (such as exporting industries) of what they would gain. Exporters and industries which would certainly gain by a reduction of tariffs, even those of their own country, have been disappointingly indifferent when their support might have been decisive."[1] Pressure of vested interests and indifference of other interests is a chief cause of the slow progress of tariff reduction whether by unilateral, bilateral, or multilateral action.

The intricacies of tariffs and the different systems adopted by the various countries have hampered the conclusion of collective agreements. Efforts in the direction of simplification and standardisation are being made, but progress is necessarily slow in view of the technical questions involved. These will certainly facilitate tariff agreements, but it should be recognised that if public opinion were strong enough, reductions could be effected even with the present complexities.

Two general hindrances to bilateral treaties and

[1] *League of Nations Official Journal, Special Supplement No. 77, Records of the Tenth Ordinary Session of the Assembly, Minutes of the Second Committee, Geneva, 1929, Annex 3.*

collective agreements merit special mention. They result from the operation of the unconditional most-favoured-nation clause and from the existence of two fundamentally different tariff policies and systems.

The grant of most-favoured-nation treatment was the general practice in Europe before the war, and its restoration in post-war commercial relations was strongly recommended by the World Economic Conference. Its unconditional grant has the advantage of avoiding discriminations and the misunderstanding and irritation to which they may lead. Thus the tariff concessions made in many of the commercial treaties negotiated in 1927 were extended to other countries by the grant of most-favoured-nation treatment. No objections are raised to the extension of such concessions to countries with lower tariffs than those of the countries concluding a treaty. In this way, British trade enjoys most-favoured-nation treatment in almost all important markets and "with relatively insignificant exceptions, British goods are admitted into foreign countries on terms at least as favourable as those applicable to similar goods imported from other foreign sources".[1]

The position is different when countries with high tariffs claim unconditional most-favoured-nation treatment. If two States have made mutual concessions by lowering tariff rates to one another and are then obliged, by the operation of the unconditional most-favoured-nation clause, to grant these concessions to other nations, the consequences may be wide and unintended. One or other of the nations making the

[1] *Final Report of the Committee on Industry and Trade*, p. 14.

F

concessions may find the expected advantages diverted to other countries which had neither incurred the work of negotiation nor made reciprocal reductions. This danger results in unwillingness to conclude bilateral treaties. It largely explains the small use made of this method since 1927.

The problem is further complicated by differences in tariff policies and systems.[1] Many countries, especially in continental Europe, have adopted the principle of establishing a tariff which is subject to negotiation and of granting lower rates by agreement concluded with one or more other States. A consequence is that higher duties may be charged on goods imported from some countries than from others. But the system has the advantage that any country can offer reciprocal concessions with a view to obtaining most-favoured-nation treatment.

Other countries fix a single tariff based on national requirements and apply it equally to all imports irrespective of the country from which they come. The tariff is not subject to reduction by subsequent bargaining. There is no discrimination against some States by the concession of privileges to others; and in return they expect no discrimination against their trade and claim most-favoured-nation treatment as a right which is beyond discussion. This system is applied chiefly by Great Britain, the United States of America, and other Anglo-Saxon countries. As already indicated,

---

[1] An analysis of the chief tariff systems is made by D. Serruys in *Commercial Treaties: Tariff Systems and Contractual Methods*, League of Nations document C.E.I. 31, Geneva 1927. Cf. also *Memorandum on European Bargaining Tariffs*, by W. T. Page (League of Nations, C.E.C.P. 97, Geneva 1927).

no difficulty need arise from this system if the tariff
levels fixed are low, as by Great Britain. Other countries
enjoy the benefit of the low duties and in return can
accord unconditional most-favoured-nation treatment.
But an awkward stalemate develops if a country
imposes a high tariff, refuses to make any adaptation
by agreement, applies it equally to all other countries,
and claims most-favoured-nation treatment from them.
Injured by the high tariff, these other countries will
be loath to grant concessions amongst themselves
which they must unconditionally extend even to
outsiders whose policy is unduly oppressive and restric-
tive to international trade. Progress in tariff reduction
is therefore seriously retarded.

These problems have been examined in detail by
the Economic Committee of the League of Nations.[1]
The Committee did not express preference either for the
system of "intangible" tariffs or for tariffs reducible by
agreement. They were of the opinion that each system
should be judged by its results. If low tariffs were fixed
little difficulty would arise; but either system might
be used harmfully and high tariffs be imposed. The
Committee emphasised that States which make reductions by agreement have often greatly exaggerated the
margin for negotiation. This practice and also that of
bringing tariffs into force and then undertaking negotiations have contributed to the establishment of unduly
high tariffs. They therefore recommended that the

[1] The Committee's discussion and conclusions on tariff systems
and their relation to most-favoured-nation treatment are given in
League of Nations document C. 138. M. 53. 1929. II, Geneva, June
1929, "Recommendations of the Economic Committee Relating
to Commercial Policy".

margin for negotiation should be narrowed, and that negotiations should precede the application of the tariffs.

On the question of "intangible" tariffs the Committee
recognised that if these are fixed with moderation there
is no reason for complaint. They were, however, of the
opinion "that the policy of those States which, having
established tariffs intolerable for other countries, refuse
to contemplate their reduction through negotiations
or otherwise . . . is incompatible with the resolutions
of the Geneva (World Economic) Conference and with
the commercial policy which it has proclaimed". The
Committee, without wishing to suggest abandonment of
the doctrine of "intangible" tariffs, were of the opinion
that when international trade is considered to suffer
thereby, assurances should be sought from countries
which take advantage of their Customs autonomy
and of their tariff liberty to raise or modify their
tariffs. They therefore suggested that such countries
should be ready to examine the representations of any
State which considered itself harmfully affected.

In considering the unconditional grant of most-
favoured-nation treatment the Economic Committee
recognised that the whole future economic work of the
League might be seriously impaired by a continuance
of the present practice. The League would find it difficult to secure multilateral agreements if States outside
an agreement could claim most-favoured-nation treatment, without themselves making any concessions. The
Committee, while not attempting to reach a final
solution, was of the opinion that the only means of
averting this danger would be to provide that States
not participating in a multilateral agreement for the

improvement of economic relations should not be entitled to claim its benefits. The benefits should, however, be granted to any State which, though not acceding to the agreement, would undertake to grant full reciprocity.

The application of mutually recognised principles for overcoming the difficulties discussed above would facilitate the conclusion of international tariff agreements. Various methods of securing progress by collective agreement are proposed and attempts have been made to put them into effect. Reference has already been made to the collective agreement on abolition of import and export prohibitions and restrictions. For dealing with tariffs the two chief methods are: (1) to arrest the upward movement by a tariff truce, i.e. an economic armistice during which plans for tariff reduction or "disarmament" might be prepared; (2) to secure agreement on a programme of reductions. It would clearly be unsatisfactory to conclude only a tariff truce as this would largely maintain the *status quo*, thus leaving wide variations in tariff levels and continuing the injury from high tariffs. Reductions would be based on a detailed study of the actual tariff levels in the different countries. They would be made by successive stages. The percentage reductions would be greatest for countries with the highest tariffs, while smaller reductions would be made by countries with intermediate or low levels. These proposals are often combined with the idea of fixing the maximum tariff level which States would undertake not to exceed. It is improbable that all countries of the world would be in a position simultaneously to undertake agreements

for reductions, but valuable results could be obtained
if a group of countries would accept a programme of
tariff reductions; the subsequent accession of other
countries could readily be arranged. The project for a
European customs agreement, which is discussed later,
is on these lines. Sometimes proposals are made for
reductions on specified commodities only; their adoption would provide experience for extension to other
commodities.[1]

ATTEMPTS TO SECURE A TARIFF TRUCE

A proposal for a tariff truce was made during the
1929 Assembly of the League of Nations by M. Hymans
(Belgium); it was strongly supported by Mr. William
Graham, President of the British Board of Trade, and
approved by the League Assembly. This led to the
so-called Tariff Truce Conference, officially designated
the Preliminary Conference with a view to Concerted
Economic Action, which was held in Geneva in February and March 1930. Thirty States were officially
represented at the Conference, twenty-seven being
European States. The results of the Conference were
meagre. Some States were unwilling to bind themselves
not to increase their tariffs even for a short period.
Owing to the lack of support the project for a real
Customs truce was abandoned. A Convention was,
however, adopted, dealing separately with countries

[1] Mention may be made of collective agreements concluded in 1928
to put an end to import and export prohibitions on hides, skins,
and bones, to abolish export duties on hides and skins, and to fix
maximum rates for export duties on bones. The agreements, which
came into force in 1929, are of interest as being the first collective
agreements on Customs matters since the war.

which conclude bilateral treaties modifying their tariff
levels by negotiation and those which fix "intangible"
tariffs.[1] States which had concluded bilateral treaties
undertook not to denounce them for a period of
one year. Also any of these States which intended to
increase its Customs duties on commodities not dealt
with in its bilateral treaties undertook to give twenty
days' notice to all other States covered by the Convention. These States, if likely to be injured by the Convention, were entitled to ask for friendly negotiations
to be opened with a view to making adjustments. If
these negotiations did not lead to a result within two
months, the State which considered itself injured
might denounce the Convention.

Countries with "intangible" tariffs, including Great
Britain, Denmark, Norway, and the Netherlands,
undertook not to increase their *protective* duties during
the validity of the Convention and recognised the
right of other signatory States to denounce the Convention if they considered themselves injured by any
increase in *fiscal* duties. Even this modest Convention failed to obtain sufficient support for effective
operation, and in March 1931 the States concerned
were unable to agree upon a date for its entry into
force.

The Conference also drew up a programme of future
negotiations for securing "closer co-operation, the
improvement of the régime of production and trade,
the enlargement of markets, and to facilitate the

[1] The text of the Convention and other decisions of the Conference
are given in League of Nations document C. 203. M. 96. 1930. II.
The League of Nations *Official Journal*, June 1930, Annex 1202,
gives a summary of the work of the Conference.

relations of the European markets between themselves and with overseas markets, so as to consolidate economic peace between the nations". Attention was directed to the need for tariff reductions and for a better organisation of production and distribution of products, with special reference to the economic relations between industrial and agricultural countries. A detailed questionnaire was drawn up on these subjects: the replies will be investigated by the Secretariat of the League of Nations as a basis for concrete proposals for closer economic co-operation especially in Europe. The programme envisaged by the Conference would therefore contribute on the economic side to the realisation of M. Briand's plan for a United States of Europe.[1]

A EUROPEAN TARIFF AGREEMENT[2]

The possibility of an agreement for tariff reductions by European countries has been much discussed during recent years. Europe is the geographical area most

[1] A Second Conference for Concerted Economic Action was held in Geneva, November 1930, when a British Government proposal was considered to secure tariff reductions by collective agreements, beginning with one or two groups of commodities, e.g. textile fabrics and machinery. This proposal was not accepted, and the Conference finally, owing to the difficulties of collective agreements, favoured bilateral negotiations instead of general action as a means for reduction of European tariffs.

[2] This subject is discussed in some detail in a Memorandum by Sir Arthur Salter on "The United States of Europe Idea" and in a Memorandum by M. Stoppani on "The Idea of a Collective Agreement to improve the Organisation of International Economic Relations in Europe", published in the League of Nations *Official Journal, Special Supplement, No. 77, Records of the Tenth Ordinary Session of the Assembly, Minutes of the Second Committee*, pp. 86 and 93.

injured by tariffs and which would benefit most from greater liberty of trading. Europe also needs economic coordination to reinforce efforts for the removal of political antagonisms. It would assist the realisation of greater security and the closer political relations which M. Briand advocates.

Europe is much interested in the idea of a customs union or a tariff agreement. This interest is based partly on the example of prosperity shown by the United States of America during post-war years. The size of the internal free trade market is recognised as an important factor in this prosperity. It is argued that similar benefit would accrue to Europe from abolition or considerable diminution of her tariff barriers. This argument has much to support it. Thus, modern methods of mass production demand large markets and the present customs units are too small to permit the best results to be derived from these methods. Europe has wide diversity of climates, natural resources, and a reasonable balance between industry and agriculture; like the United States of America, therefore, she has all the elements required for a well-balanced economic unit. Also many of her countries are industrially mature.

But closer economic unity in Europe is supported not only from a desire to imitate the United States of America; it is based in part on hostility to her trans-Atlantic rival. There is resentment against American tariff and migration policies, and fear of the growing flood of American exports of manufactured goods and of the domination of American capital. It would indeed be unfortunate if this hostility, by diverting attention from Europe's real need, led to higher tariffs against the United States instead of lower internal tariffs in Europe.

Reduction of tariffs between the European countries demands much preparatory work both in the establishment of general principles and in the detailed study of the often highly complicated tariffs now in force. It is desirable that the work of preparation should be undertaken through the League of Nations and not independently. In evolving general principles of agreement the frequent and regular meeting of Ministers of Commerce and of Agriculture would be of great value, along similar lines to the meeting of Foreign Ministers on the Council of the League of Nations. This is emphasised strongly by Sir Arthur Salter in his Memorandum on the idea of a United States of Europe.[1]

In drafting a programme of reduction, allowance must be made for the fact that the present European tariffs range from very high to very low levels. For countries with low levels only minor adjustments for a few commodities would be necessary. Also countries with the highest tariffs would be expected to make proportionately greater reductions than those with intermediate levels. The reductions would be made gradually by successive and, as far as possible, simultaneous stages during a period of one or two decades. Each country might be left free to make in its own way the percentage reductions agreed upon, subject, however, to provisions preventing the changes from being merely nominal by large reductions of non-protective duties on goods not produced in the country

---

[1] See footnote [2] on page 88.

or the import of which is small, while retaining the
really important protective duties unaltered. Any
disputes which might arise on these or other questions
could be referred to arbitration, the procedure for
which could be included in the agreement for tariff
reduction.

To be effective it is not essential that all European
countries should join in an agreement for tariff reductions. It might be inaugurated by a group of adjacent
States and subsequently extended by the entry of
other States. On the other hand, the agreement need
not be limited to European countries. It could be open
to any country which undertook to observe its conditions.

What should be the tariff policy of States within
the agreement to those outside? It would be impossible
to secure agreement for tariff reduction by any considerable number of European States if the reductions
would be automatically granted to all States outside
the agreement by the unconditional operation of the
most-favoured-nation clause. The proposal most discussed is mutually to reduce tariffs for countries in
the agreement while maintaining the present levels on
imports from other countries. Some concessions might,
however, be granted. The deciding factor seems to be
the tariff levels of the States outside the agreement,
whether in Europe or not. Thus a country which for
any reason was not able formally to join the agreement,
but which had tariffs corresponding with the lowest
levels in the agreement might reasonably expect and
might readily be granted the same tariff scales as the
signatories of the agreement practised amongst them-

selves. Thus Great Britain, so long as she maintains
her present tariff levels, which are the lowest in the
world, might reasonably be allowed to benefit from
the reductions even if she did not join the agreement.
These privileges might, however, be withdrawn if a
country benefiting in this way changed her policy and
raised her tariff levels. This position might arise if
Great Britain established a general system of Empire
preferences.

The position is different where a country outside
the agreement has high tariffs. Such a country could
not reasonably claim the benefit of reductions under
the agreement while retaining its own high duties.
Nor would the States in the agreement be likely to
make this concession. They might undertake not to
raise their tariffs against non-signatory countries
unless, perhaps, after these countries had imposed
still higher tariffs. But States with high tariffs outside
the agreement would have no complaint if they did
not receive unconditional most-favoured-nation treatment and were subject to discrimination.

The countries chiefly affected would be the United
States of America and certain of the self-governing
countries of the British Commonwealth. It is essential
that their sympathetic understanding and not their
resentment against an agreement for tariff reduction
should be secured. If the agreement permitted the
United States of America or any other country to
join provided it observed the same conditions as the
States in the agreement, there could be no legitimate
feeling of irritation. European countries do not resent
the fact that free trade is established between Massa-

chusetts, Texas, California, and all the other States in
the United States of America, but denied to the outside
world. The United States of America would have still
less ground for resentment as she would be free to
join the Customs agreement. Her remedy would rest
in her own hands. She could secure all the benefits by
offering reciprocity. Even if she preferred to retain her
high tariffs she would derive advantage from increase
of Europe's purchasing power in world markets which
would result from the Customs agreement. This is
already recognised by American business men who are
definitely favourable to closer economic coordination
between European countries.

Although, up to the present, even in Europe the
movement for reducing tariff barriers has met with
no outstanding success, there is an accumulation of
opinion in its support which should lead to practical
results. Support for the principle of greater liberty
of trading is forthcoming from Governments and from
organisations representative of commerce, industry,
and labour. The International Chamber of Commerce,
in anticipation of the World Economic Conference,
expressed the conviction that "excessive Customs
duties, the instability and constant increases in Customs
tariffs constitute the most serious barriers to international trade; and that a complete change in the
tendencies of existing opinion is necessary". Even
the American Committee of the Chamber, basing their
conclusion on the value of absence of trade barriers
throughout the United States, "felt that substantially
similar freedom of commerce and trade in Europe

would inevitably result in great benefit to the European peoples".[1] They refrained, however, from taking the further step of extolling the benefits of free trade between Europe and the United States!

On the labour side the International Federation of Trade Unions included the promotion of international trade in its Economic Policy, formulated in 1929, and reiterated its demand "for the abolition of tariff and Customs barriers, which constitute a great obstacle to the restoration of healthy world economic conditions and especially for the abolition of such barriers in Europe; the abolition of import and export prohibitions by international conventions; and uniformity in the general provisions of commercial treaties".[2] It is unnecessary to repeat the recommendations of the World Economic Conference in favour of tariff reductions. These were accepted by the various interests represented at the Conference—employers, workers, traders, and Governments. They have subsequently been unanimously endorsed by the Government delegates from more than fifty nations in the Assembly of the League of Nations.

The measure of agreement on the principle is in marked contrast with the failure of attempts to translate it into practice. There are signs, admittedly still very indistinct, that protection has reached its zenith and there is reason to expect the beginning of a movement towards freer trade in the future. It was inevitable that the first decade after the greatest war in history

[1] *Final Report of the Trade Barriers Committee of the International Chamber of Commerce*, League of Nations document C.E.I. 5 (1), Geneva, 1927.
[2] *The International Trade Union Movement*, October 1929, p. 197.

should be marked by high protectionism based on national antagonisms and economic chaos. The next decade may see the development of a greater feeling of national security and mutual confidence between the nations. This is the essential basis of tariff reductions. Economic conditions are more stable and special measures of protection, necessary until recently, are no longer required. With the cessation of currency inflation, "exchange dumping" is no longer important, and measures taken against it can be withdrawn. Various import and export prohibitions established during the war or in the early post-war years are gradually being removed.

During recent years the chief tariff increases have been by the United States, Canada, Australia, and other extra-European countries. Many of the newer overseas countries will show no tendency for tariff reductions until their industrial development has made considerable progress. In the United States, however, further increases beyond the high level of the 1930 tariff are improbable, and the future tendency is likely to be gradually downwards. To the surprise of many Americans the raising of the tariff in 1930, far from restoring industrial prosperity, coincided with a deepening of the depression. Many large-scale American manufacturers, desiring to develop their export trade, will exert increasing influence for lower tariffs. There is also a growing sensitiveness to European opinion. These forces can work only slowly. High protection has been preached and practised for so many years that it will not readily be renounced. Also the increase in welfare of the United States from low tariffs would be small compared with that which Europe would derive from a diminution of her many tariffs. Nevertheless, there begin to be indications in the United States of wavering in the confidence with which high tariffs are advocated.

In Europe tariff levels have risen little during the last three or four years. Low tariffs have been maintained by the countries of North-Western Europe. In December 1930 a Conference was held in Oslo, attended by representatives of Norway, Sweden, Denmark, the Netherlands, Belgium, and Luxemburg, and a Convention for economic rapprochement was adopted. The Conference also proposed further negotiations between the Governments of the States represented, with a view to reducing barriers to trade and facilitating international commerce. A disposition to negotiate bilateral commercial treaties is being shown, especially by some of the States of Central and South-Eastern Europe. Desire for closer economic cooperation is one of the chief bases of the proposal for a "United States of Europe". Strong, persistent leadership is needed to coordinate these tendencies towards saner international trade relations. Their realisation would increase material welfare and, by strengthening world economic unity instead of isolated economic nationalism, would greatly facilitate the maintenance of peace.

CHAPTER V

INTERNATIONAL ORGANISATION OF PRODUCTION AND TRADE

In the preceding chapters greater liberty of trading was advocated as a means of securing more efficient use of the world's productive resources. Tariffs were regarded as an obstacle to securing maximum efficiency. High tariffs especially were considered to represent the power of vested interests against the general welfare; they were also seen to be an expression of exaggerated nationalism or of absence of international security.

Condemnation of tariffs is not a vindication of *laissez-faire*. Intense competition often involves serious waste. Maximum efficiency in production and commerce will be attained neither by tariffs nor *laissez-faire*. It demands cooperation between producers, traders, and consumers, and to give the best results this cooperation must not be limited by political frontiers. Organised economic internationalism, especially for the staple commodities of trade, is needed to secure the greatest material welfare and to establish the foundations for world peace.

During the nineteenth century unrestricted competition between producers was predominant. This gave reasonably satisfactory results so long as markets were easy to secure. Manufacturing establishments were relatively small and there was wide variety of products. Steadily, however, the size of undertakings in many industries has increased, whether by growth

G

or by amalgamations, and variety of products has been reduced by standardisation. Also association and cooperation have been established by working arrangements between formerly competing units, and these have often been strengthened by financial interrelations. The United States of America led the way in consolidations or trusts, while Germany elaborated the cartel type of association between independent companies. In Great Britain and other countries consolidations and combines have grown steadily in importance.[1] The process of combination has been accelerated in recent years.

Two chief motives have been responsible for these changes: (1) to avoid the wastes of competition, and (2) to secure the economies of large-scale manufacture. Associations and amalgamations have been formed for the first of these objects especially during periods of depression when competition is exceptionally severe with demand below capacity to produce. Competing companies, in their endeavour to secure markets, engage in price wars aimed at the destruction of their rivals. These wars are often long and involve international bitterness and also loss of capital from the failure of firms. It is true that the consumer receives some benefit in low prices, but this may be outweighed by instability of supply and wide fluctuation in prices. Also production by small competing units often involves higher costs than by cooperation and amalgamation.

[1] An account of consolidations and associations in Great Britain is given in the reports of the Committee on Industry and Trade. Cf. also the Ministry of Reconstruction's *Report of Committee on Trusts*, Cd. 9236, London, 1919.

It is unnecessary to discuss in detail the economies which may result from cooperation between small units or from the development of large undertakings. They include economies in the purchase of raw materials and the sale of the finished product. Overhead charges per unit of output are reduced and overlapping of sales organisations and competitive advertising avoided. The product can often be standardised and plant specialised. A large unit or an association of small units can promote technical research. Information about the probable trend of demand can be compiled and production adjusted to the requirements of the market. New capital developments can be made systematically to meet expansion of demand.[1]

With these various objects consolidation and cooperation have made rapid progress *within* the different countries. The national industries have consequently been strengthened. But, though greater internal stability has been attained, international competition has become more intense. This has been marked by

[1] The favourable results of international industrial agreements are well summarised in the Report of the World Economic Conference which was of the opinion that "in certain branches of production they can—subject to certain conditions and reservations—on the one hand, secure a more methodical organisation of production and a reduction in costs by means of a better utilisation of existing equipment, the development on more suitable lines of new plant, and a more rational grouping of undertakings, and, on the other hand, act as a check on uneconomic competition and reduce the evils resulting from fluctuations in industrial activity.

By this means they may assure to the workers greater stability of employment and at the same time, by reducing production and distribution costs and consequently selling prices, bring advantages to the consumer." *First Report*, p. 41. The menace of monopoly to which the Conference also called attention is discussed in a later section.

price wars to capture or retain foreign markets, dumping abroad with higher prices at home, protective tariffs and subsidies. World productive resources have been used uneconomically, industries artificially maintained in countries for which they are not well suited, standards of living adversely affected, and international relations strained. Attempts have been made to avoid these difficulties and to secure the advantages of cooperation by extending association and consolidation of production and trade into the international field. Some success has been achieved, but the movement is still in its initial stages and there is scope for much progress.

DEVELOPMENT OF INTERNATIONAL ORGANISATION

Already before the war trusts and cartels had expanded into the international field. Germany, having led the way in establishing national cartels, was prominent in the formation of international agreements. Most of these collapsed during the war, but many have since been resumed. The movement has also extended to branches of industry not covered by pre-war agreements, and there is a tendency for international cartels to increase in number and importance. Some cartels are merely agreements between representatives of an industry in only two or three neighbouring countries. Several such agreements have been concluded since 1919 between producers formerly in association in the same country, but now separated by the new national frontiers drawn up by the Peace Treaties. Other agreements have a larger membership. The commodities covered include steel, rails, pipes, wire and other metal products, wagons, incandescent lamps, electric lamps, certain chemicals, sugar, and enamel goods.[1] Frequently cartels and trusts are formed in industries in which capital equipment is important and in which consequently the losses from over-development and severe competition would be serious.

Cartels vary considerably in the closeness of association established between the national groups and in their objects. Many are undertakings by each participant to refrain from competing in the home markets of other participants. Thus, by the Franco-German Potash Agreement the French market is reserved for French producers and the German market for German producers. Also, as about 95 per cent. of the world's potash is produced by these two countries, the Agreement provides for joint effort to educate potential purchasers in the use of potash fertilisers.

Very few agreements fix minimum selling prices. More frequently, however, export quotas are fixed or markets allotted, while sometimes agreement is reached on total output and a proportion of this is allotted to each member country. Thus the wagon manufacturers of continental Europe, at a meeting in Berlin on April 24, 1930, reached an agreement on export

[1] The development of cartels and trusts and the international problems involved are discussed in various memoranda submitted to the World Economic Conference, including those by Professors Grossman, MacGregor, de Rousiers, and Wiedenfeld; League of Nations documents C.E.C.P. 24 (1), 93, 95, and 57 (1).

In December 1930 the League of Nations published a review consisting of a series of monographs on the rôle and working of various international agreements, document P. 1930. II. 41. See also *The United States of Europe*, by Edouard Herriot, London, 1930.

quotas with a view to avoiding competition in the
export market. The quotas fixed were as follows:

	Per cent.		Per cent.
Belgium	34·6	Czechoslovakia ..	6·9
Germany	28·8	Hungary	2·4
France	13·9	Austria	2·2
Italy	10·5	Switzerland ..	0·7

An important example of a cartel regulating output
is the International Steel Agreement, concluded in
September 1926 between France, Belgium, Germany,
and Luxemburg. Other continental countries, including
Poland and Czechoslovakia, subsequently joined. The
plan adopted was for a Central Board to estimate the
total tonnage which the market would require and to
allot to each country a fixed quota of this total. Each
country was required to pay into a common fund a
dollar for each ton of crude steel produced. A country
which exceeded its quota paid into the fund four
dollars per ton of excess. If a country's output was less
than its quota it received from the fund two dollars
for each ton of deficit. At intervals the balance in
the fund was distributed mainly in proportion to the
production of each country. The original terms of the
Agreement were subsequently modified.[1]

Cartels are usually loose associations without any
close financial relation. In many industries, however,
international trusts have developed with manufacturing establishments in different countries. These trusts

[1] In the autumn of 1930 difficulties in the working of the agreement almost led to a breakdown.

are great businesses with close financial connection. They differ considerably in their origin and structure. Some, for example the Ford Motor Company, have grown from a strong undertaking in one country which has developed large foreign markets and has then found it convenient to set up factories abroad instead of concentrating production at home. Among many advantages are reduction in costs of transportation, the avoidance of tariffs by producing within the Customs walls of the various countries, specialisation of plant and increase of production in countries where conditions are most favourable and labour costs lowest.

Other international trusts have been established by the permanent fusion or financial association of formerly competing companies with establishments in different countries. The Swedish Match Company has developed partly by fusion with companies in other countries and partly by securing from the Governments of certain countries monopoly rights for the production and sale of matches for a period of years in return for loans. Among other well-known trusts are the Standard Oil and Royal Dutch groups which control 40 per cent. of the world's production of petroleum and are predominant in its international trade. Many other international trusts have been established for a wide range of commodities, including meat, margarine, tobacco, radiators, sewing cotton, artificial silk, soap, and chemicals. They range from complete fusions and companies with branch establishments or subsidiaries in different countries to holding companies and cooperation based on interchange of shares and interlocking directorates, all of which provide means for regulating and stabilising international production and trade.

Cartels and trusts limit their operations mainly to a single commodity or industry. These are not, however, the only possibilities of international organisation of production and trade. Other developments are indicated by the proposals under consideration in Central and Eastern Europe to increase facilities for the exchange of agricultural and industrial products, by economic aspects of the project for a United States of Europe and by plans for British Empire economic cooperation on the lines discussed at the Imperial Conference, 1930. They include proposals for the regulation of trade by agreement upon marketing methods, import quotas, and bulk purchase of staple products. On the side of production the object would be to plan capital developments so that the economic structure of different countries will be complementary rather than competitive.

These developments may be so far-reaching that they will require the participation not only of producers and merchants, but also of consumers, labour, and Governments. They will involve delicate and detailed negotiations, but they offer large possibilities of economy in capital and productive effort and of improvement of international relations. They cannot, of course, prevent a country from developing certain industries which it considers necessary for its welfare even if this involves increased competition and uneconomic utilisation of capital. But each country has alternative lines of development some of which fit in better than others with productive trends abroad. These offer a basis for negotiation and agreement. The best results will be obtained only if the principle of refraining from discrimination against other countries is observed.

EFFECTS ON INTERNATIONAL COMPETITION

International cartels, trusts, and other forms of organisation and cooperation may be judged by their effect in diminishing the intensity of economic conflict and by the extent to which they cut across political frontiers and permit of the rational economic organisation of industry. These frontiers are essentially artificial and obstructive for the economic world. They should present the minimum obstacle to productive organisation and trade if maximum efficiency in the use of the world's economic resources is to be secured.

Cartels are often mainly means of protecting the producers of each country by securing the home market from foreign competition. They thus represent a nationalist conception, and their effect is very similar to that of protective tariffs.[1] In fact, they have the same effect as a prohibition of imports of the commodity concerned. They thus prevent producers in countries able to produce at the lowest costs from extending their sales to the home markets of other member-countries.

Cartels of this type have, nevertheless, advantages

[1] It is sometimes argued that cartels would reduce the demand for tariffs, but this is unlikely, especially if they do not cover all producing countries.

The League Economic Consultative Committee stated in its report immediately prior to the 1929 Assembly that "cartels have tended to stabilise rather than modify the tariff position". (*Minutes of the Second Committee of the 1929 Assembly*, page 81.)

over tariffs. Tariffs are imposed by the isolated action
of each country, or at best are the result of bargains
embodied in commercial treaties. The atmosphere
surrounding tariff legislation is one of conflict and
opposition. It is true that cartels are often formed only
after bitter competition, and that during the negotiations each member endeavours to secure the best
terms. But a cartel is superior to tariffs in being an
agreement between producers. It establishes personal
relations between the leaders of industry in the different
countries.

An international cartel may hinder expansion in the
production of the commodity concerned by countries
with the lowest costs. This danger is probably not
considerable. The producers of such a country would
not join a cartel if they had reasonable prospect of
extending their markets by continuing competition.
The position is different if a number of countries have
reached fair stability in the extent of their markets
based on selling prices which allow reasonable profits
and if attempts by any country to expand its markets
by general price-cutting or by dumping would result
in similar measures by other countries. In these
circumstances an agreement to maintain the *status quo*
would be generally advantageous and would have
reasonable prospect of durability. If an agreement
had the effect of injuring the interests of the more
efficient countries, the terms might be revised in their
favour; otherwise they might be tempted to withdraw
and resume unrestricted competition.

As has been seen, some cartels go beyond agreements
merely to reserve the home market for the home

producer. Allocation of markets between the different members avoids the losses of cut-throat competition. Here, again, a cartel is likely to be established only where competition would result rather in exhaustion of all the combatants than in decisive victory for some of them. Allocation of markets will be based mainly on the *status quo*, but some adjustment may be made to avoid unnecessary transportation.

Where a cartel fixes total output and the quota of each country, a high degree of coordination has been reached. Difficulties arise in fixing the quotas, especially where there is considerable variation in the proportionate output of each country during several years prior to the agreement. Also changes in quotas are often the occasion for dispute as countries claim increases in their proportion of total output. During the operation of an agreement the system of imposing fines on countries exceeding their quota and of paying "bonuses" to countries producing less than their quota allows some elasticity by enabling the more progressive countries to expand their production, though they suffer the penalty of the fine for doing so.

Although hitherto international cartels have been based mainly on the nationalist conception and organisation of production and trade they have at least restricted competition by mutual agreement. Also the system is capable of considerable development. Restriction of competition has resulted in increased willingness by producers in different countries to exchange experience and patents and to cooperate in research. Closer links might be established which would enable specialisation of production to be practised. Also, though hitherto cartels have been controlled by producers only, a future development may make possible the association of consumers and workers in their administration.

International trusts have advantages over cartels by breaking across the nationalist organisation of production and trade. The factories of a trust in different countries cooperate instead of competing with one another. Expansion of output in countries which have superior advantages in production, even if accompanied by decline in others, is not the result of an international struggle, but of a rational policy based on records of costings and facilities for marketing. The prosperity of the whole organisation is increased, though the scale of production of some of its national units may decline.

The development of international trusts does not imply the elimination of competition. Only rarely does an international trust control the whole or so large a proportion of the production that it constitutes a world monopoly. It is usually in competition with other international trusts or with national producers. The essential point, however, is that competition is largely, or entirely, excluded between its own components throughout the world, and that its competition with other producers is not a conflict between national units.

Extension of the productive, commercial, and financial structure of international trusts over a large number of countries is of value not only in establishing closer economic relations but in strengthening the foundations of peace. An international agreement between national cartels can easily break up in time of war. But an international trust with interests in many countries would suffer serious disorganisation and loss in the event of war, and its influence would therefore be exerted for the maintenance of peace.

THE MENACE OF MONOPOLY

International cartels and trusts, though of value in reducing the severity of international competition and in ensuring greater stability and regularity of production and trade, involve the risks of monopoly power. An international cartel is built up of national groups each able to control the whole or a very large part of national production. A great international trust, though rarely a world monopoly, often has monopoly power in some areas. This power may be exercised against consumers and against the workers.

The menace of monopoly and means of combating it have been widely discussed. Thus the Trade Barriers Committee of the International Chamber of Commerce, while recognising the value of international industrial agreements in replacing ruinous competition by international cooperation and in lowering costs, "insists upon the necessity of safeguarding the interests of labour, of commerce, and of the public".[1] On similar lines the World Economic Conference saw the danger of abuses and the need for measures to prevent them.

The exercise of monopoly power by an international cartel or trust affects the consumer mainly through selling price. The formation of a cartel after a severe price war may be followed by a rise in price. This may

[1] *Final Report of the Committee*, C.E.I. 5 (1), Geneva, 1927, p. 37.

be reasonable if competition had forced prices down to an uneconomic level. Apart from these circumstances the consumer has the right to expect that the economies of coordinated organisation will result in lower prices than would prevail under the more wasteful methods of competition and smaller scale production. Yet experience has frequently shown that those responsible for the direction of monopolies, whether national or international, have been too ready to snatch at monopoly profits based on restriction of output and high selling prices. Sometimes they have even neglected to use the opportunities afforded them to reduce costs of production. Protected from competition, they have shown little energy in improving their productive efficiency; methods of organisation have been inferior and the rate of technical progress slower than with the stimulus of healthy competition.

The use of monopoly power to raise prices to consumers may cause bitterness between producing and consuming countries. A differential selling policy with higher prices to consumers in some countries would be especially objectionable.

Frequently the exercise of monopoly power against the interests of consumers and workers brings its own Nemesis. Consumers will endeavour to protect themselves by forming buyers' associations. They will turn to the use of substitutes. Also monopolies are rarely complete and restriction of output and artificial raising of prices stimulate competition from outside, or may tempt some of the more efficient producers in a cartel to revert to free competition. These risks should lead persons responsible for directing the policy of international cartels and trusts to exercise their power with moderation. The events of recent years in the control of production or price of various commodities, e.g. rubber and copper, are a sufficient indication of the difficulty of attempting to secure large monopoly revenues by fixing an unduly high selling price.[1]

Although abuse of monopoly power often brings its own penalty, this does not afford adequate protection of the public interests. The abuse may continue for a considerable period during which injury is inflicted on the community. Consequently a number of countries have passed legislation making certain monopolistic practices illegal and providing for investigation and even control to prevent abuses. This legislation and experience of its operation suggest the chief features of any international system of regulation which may be set up.

In Great Britain there is no special legislation governing trusts and cartels; they are subject to the common law doctrine on restraint of trade, but this has interfered little with their development. In 1919 the Committee on Trusts recommended that permanent machinery should be set up to investigate the operation of monopolies, trusts, and combines. The Committee also expressed the opinion that it would be found necessary ultimately to establish further machinery for dealing with abuses revealed by investigation. No machinery for these purposes has yet been established.

[1] Mr. J. W. F. Rowe's article in the *Economic Journal*, September, 1930, on "The Artificial Control of Raw Material Supplies" illustrates the practical value of organisation and control, and also the dangers which arise if producers short-sightedly fix high monopoly prices. See also B. B. Wallace and L. R. Edminster, *International Control of Raw Materials*, Washington, 1930.

In the United States the Clayton Act of 1914 makes illegal various practices, including the holding by one company of shares in another, which result in a real diminution of competition between companies or tend to establish a monopoly. Unjustified discriminations towards different customers are also illegal. In the same year the Federal Trade Commission was set up to examine and report to Congress on practices which infringe the Clayton and other anti-trust laws and to prevent unfair competition. The Commission can also offer advice on methods of association and operation which would bring organisations into conformity with the legislation. In several British Dominions, especially Canada, legislative provision is made for the investigation of combines, monopolies, and trusts. In Canada, penalties may be imposed for the formation of combines detrimental to the public welfare, while patent rights and customs tariffs which have facilitated the operations of a combine may be withdrawn.

German legislation is favourable to the formation of combines; in one or two industries cartels have even been formed compulsorily by the public authorities. The State has powers of investigation and supervision to prevent abuse of economic power by cartels. Norway has a system for the control of combines. This aims at preventing limitation of competition and improper manipulation of prices. Combines for regulating prices, production, or marketing must register with an Office of Control. All relevant information on business methods must be disclosed to the control officials, who have the right to examine the books and papers of any combine. Powers are provided for dissolving associations which regulate competition in ways contrary to the good of the public, for cancelling any arrangements which have this effect, and for preventing unreasonable price differentiation.[1]

Rôle of the League of Nations

The League of Nations may (1) coordinate national action and itself take steps to prevent abuses by international cartels and trusts; (2) facilitate agreements for the better regulation of production and trade, especially in industries where competition is severe and harmful.

Coordination of national action for the prevention of abuses is complicated by differences in the attitude and policy of the various Governments to cartels and trusts. National laws and administrations have jurisdiction not merely over national cartels and trusts but generally also over international cartels and trusts operating within the country. It is essential, therefore, to establish agreed principles if the application of conflicting policies is to be avoided. This involves a detailed study of national law and practice. The League has already published reviews of these legal aspects of industrial agreements, and also on economic aspects of several international agreements.[2]

But the League has a more direct rôle in the prevention of abuses. Its chief weapon is publicity. It should therefore make comprehensive studies on the

[1] Further details about these and other countries are given in a *Review of Legislation on Cartels and Trusts*, submitted to the World Economic Conference, C.E.I. 35.
[2] League of Nations documents P. 1930. II. 11 and 41.

lines recommended by the World Economic Conference into the methods, technical progress, and price policy of international cartels and trusts. These economic studies should be completed by investigations into working conditions by the International Labour Office. As the World Economic Conference pointed out, such studies would not only tend to prevent the growth of abuses, but would secure the support of public opinion for agreements which conduce to the general interest.

Whether regulation and control by the League will become necessary depends on the policy adopted by international cartels and trusts. If they effect economies and lower costs of production, establish fair labour conditions, fix reasonable selling prices in relation to costs and avoid discriminations, the only action by the League will be one of encouragement. If, however, abuses arise, the League should cooperate with national Governments for the protection of the public interest. Proposals have already been made that international cartels and trusts should be required to register with the League and that the League should exercise permanent supervision over them.[1] Special arrangements would be necessary for the investigation of abuses. These would include the establishment of (1) a recognised channel for complaints and demands by a national Government or a responsible international body for enquiry into alleged abuses; (2) general principles of procedure and methods of investigation.

[1] The Inter-Parliamentary Union passed a resolution on these lines at its Conference in London, July 1930. The International Federation of Trade Unions includes in its economic policy a proposal for the effective supervision of international trusts, cartels, and combines by the Economic Organisation of the League of Nations.

One method would be for the investigations and subsequent action to be conducted by national Governments with coordination by the League. If experience
showed this method to be unsatisfactory, enquiries by
an international committee could be undertaken. An
ad hoc committee for each enquiry would be necessary
to ensure the inclusion of persons with intimate knowledge of the conditions of production and trade in
the industry under investigation. Committees might,
however, include a permanent nucleus of persons
experienced in the general problems and methods of
investigation involved. Committees would also receive
assistance from members of the League Secretariat
who had specialised in the study of trusts and cartels.

As already indicated, the League's rôle is wider
than merely to assist in preventing abuses by international cartels and trusts. It includes the positive
task of facilitating discussions between all those
interested, whether as producers or consumers, in
industries suffering from extreme international competition. Mention has been made of the waste of capital
and productive effort which such competition entails.
It embitters international relations and, as discussed
in the following chapter, it involves strain on industrial
relations by leading to competition in labour standards.
These harmful consequences could be largely, if not
altogether, avoided by agreements on output, markets,
and labour standards. Yet circumstances sometimes
make it difficult for discussions to be undertaken and
agreements reached on the initiative of representatives
of the industry alone. Here the League may have opportunities for bringing together the parties concerned to

discuss their problems in an impartial atmosphere with a view to securing international cooperation.

On these lines the Economic Committee of the League has begun a study of international aspects of the coal problem. Facts have been compiled which show that the industry is suffering from a capacity to produce which far exceeds the demand for coal. This has led to "a struggle between the exporting countries to secure new markets or to maintain old ones, and an endeavour by others to ward off the attacks of foreign competition by entrenching themselves behind protective barriers or to surmount barriers erected elsewhere by employing commercial methods anti-economic in character".[1]

The weakness of the industry is that it is in the interests of each individual producer to fight for any business he can get, though this is to the detriment of producers as a whole. National measures to strengthen the national industry and increase its production by subsidies, preferential railway rates, tariffs, dumping, wage reductions, and increasing the hours of work have been countered by similar measures in other countries. The effect has been to aggravate the fundamental difficulty.[2]

In establishing the facts and discussing the problems the Economic Committee during 1929 organised meet-

[1] *The Problem of the Coal Industry: Interim Report on its International Aspects by the Economic Committee of the League of Nations.* Geneva, 1929. (C. 150. M. 58. 1929. II, page 10.)

[2] A valuable recent account of the position of the British Coal Trade in relation to this welter of competition is given by Professor J. H. Jones in a paper read before the Royal Statistical Society, November 19, 1929. (*Journal of the Royal Statistical Society*, Part I, 1930.)

ings, first of experts on the owners' side, then of labour experts, and subsequently a joint meeting. The interests of consuming countries were also represented. In its Interim Report the Economic Committee stated that "almost all the experts agreed that the problem as it affects Europe has international elements, a comprehension of which is essential to its solution".[1] Among international remedies which received almost unanimous support of the experts, both of the employers and the miners, was that international agreements between producers should be arranged to regulate output, exports, markets, or prices. Only by these means could orderly production and sale be achieved and the industry restored on a sound financial basis.[2]

The countries essential to the success of an agreement are few in number. They are Great Britain, France, Belgium, Germany, Poland, and one or two other European countries. The United States is a large producer of coal, but for geographical reasons it is not in severe competition with the European countries.

For such an agreement it is necessary that the industry in each country should be nationally organised. If, for example, an agreement were reached on the total output of the participating countries and on the

---

[1] *Interim Report*, p. 13.

[2] Other proposals were the abolition of artificial restrictions to trade in coal and artificial stimuli to production, the setting up of a special international committee representative of all interests (Governments, employers, miners, merchants, and consumers) to study and regulate the industry, and the establishment of an international agreement on hours, wages, and social conditions. Progress on the last of these proposals has been made by the International Labour Organisation, a Draft Convention on hours of labour being under discussion by the 1930 and 1931 Sessions of the International Labour Conference.

quota of each country, some organisation would be required in each country to guarantee that the quota would be observed and to distribute it among the different districts and colliery companies. The chief coal-producing countries of continental Europe were already organised in this way at the time of the Economic Committee's Interim Report in 1929, but Great Britain had no national body which could undertake the obligations involved. This obstacle has, however, since been overcome by the machinery set up under the Coal Mines Act, 1930. In accordance with the provisions of this Act a Central Council, consisting of representatives of the owners in the various districts, has been set up mainly to allocate to each district its maximum output during specified periods. With this machinery Great Britain is now equipped to take part in an international agreement for the regulation of output.

It is still uncertain that an agreement to regulate output or markets will be reached between the chief European coal-producing countries. Up to the present the discussions have been very tentative. However, by bringing representatives of the industry together for these discussions, the League has already made a useful contribution, and it will have further opportunities for facilitating negotiations with a view to agreements for eliminating unfair and severe competition. In this and other industries the League will be likely to avoid directly promoting agreements, but will leave the initiative to representatives of the industry.

The rôle of the League is not limited to facilitating

discussions in single industries engaged in severe international competition. It can assist countries in establishing economic cooperation on the wider basis already indicated of complementary instead of competitive developments of production and trade. Frequent international meetings of Ministers of Commerce and of business men would be of value for this purpose as well as for the gradual diminution of tariff barriers and other obstacles to international trade. They would help in developing permanent international machinery to remove the harmful effects of unregulated competition.

CHAPTER VI

INTERNATIONAL REGULATION OF LABOUR STANDARDS

Side by side with improvements in the international regulation of production and trade on the lines discussed in the preceding chapter there is need for international regulation of labour standards. A country's standards of labour conditions depend primarily on its productive efficiency and system of distribution. This enables a highly efficient country to maintain high labour standards alongside low standards abroad. But there is continuous interaction between the standards of different countries through the medium of international trade. The effects are felt especially by industries producing for foreign markets or industries exposed to the competition of foreign products in the home market. If in such an industry labour standards in one country are unduly low, the standards of other countries are menaced or undermined. This causes industrial conflict and international bitterness. Its prevention is essential for the promotion both of industrial and of international peace.

Conflict in labour standards is especially bitter as it affects the standard of living of large masses of the population in each country. It is indeed a conflict of peoples. Demands for increases in wages or reductions of hours in one country are refused because of the low standards in competing countries abroad. Reductions in labour standards first in one country and then in another follow from severe competition for markets.

Before the war British workers were continually told that their standards could not be raised while German standards were so much lower. Since the war the argument is used in many countries that unemployment and low labour standards are due to the unfair wages and unduly long hours worked abroad. Such conditions breed resentment between the peoples of the world which, in moments of political tension, contributes to the outbreak of war.

National action alone is powerless; only by international measures can these conditions be remedied. Action is desired in the field of labour standards for two closely related reasons—to ensure reasonable conditions to the workers on humanitarian grounds, and to prevent unfair competition. On the humanitarian side efforts should be concentrated on raising the standards of the most backward countries and of trades in which sweating prevails in the more advanced countries. The abolition of the semi-slavery of native labour in colonial areas and the suppression of child labour and excessive hours of work in some of the Asiatic countries are examples of action urgently demanded on humanitarian grounds. Also, in some of the European countries sweated labour, based especially on unduly low wages, is far too common.

Elimination of competition based on unfair labour conditions is especially necessary as a measure of economic disarmament. Healthy competition under fair conditions provides a stimulus to efficiency, whereas unfair competition inevitably results in menace to international relations. Not only is ill-will created but international trade is hampered by tariff barriers erected to afford protection against unfair foreign competition.

The need for international action to regulate labour standards has long been recognised. Over a century ago Robert Owen saw some of the possibilities. During the second half of the nineteenth century the trade unions and also socialist organisations came to realise that isolated efforts in each country to maintain or improve labour conditions and standards of living were seriously hampered by lower standards abroad. When workers in some countries were forced to accept lower wages and longer hours, the effects were soon felt in other countries. Only by united action could coordinated progress be made. The Socialists and the Trade Unionists of many of the European countries therefore organised a series of international conferences to draw up principles and programmes and to co-ordinate their policies. During the closing years of the nineteenth century the Governments of some of the chief European countries began to consider the reper-cussions of international competition on standards of labour conditions. In 1890 an official conference held in Berlin and attended by representatives of fourteen countries passed a series of resolutions on conditions of labour in mines, provision of a weekly rest day, and regulation of child labour. About ten years later the International Association for Labour Legislation was formed to study the development of labour legislation in different countries and to promote international agreements on labour conditions. The Association was a private organisation, but several Governments took an active interest in its work. Its most notable achievement was the adoption of an international convention to prohibit the use of white phosphorus in the manufacture of matches.[1]

These activities were largely interrupted by the war, but were resumed and much developed after its termination. The workers became increasingly active through the International Federation of Trade Unions, while the employers established an international Confederation to coordinate the activities of the national groups. But the chief advance over the pre-war position has been the establishment under the Peace Treaties of the International Labour Organisation in which Governments, employers, and workers are officially associated for the removal of social injustice and the adoption of humane conditions of labour. The authors of the Peace Treaties recognised that "the failure of any nation to adopt humane conditions of labour is an obstacle in the way of other nations which desire to improve the conditions in their own countries". They admitted that "conditions of labour exist involving such injustice, hardship, and privation to large numbers of people as to produce unrest so great that the peace and harmony of the world are imperilled".[2] They saw the urgent need for an improvement of these conditions and therefore agreed to set up the International Labour Organisation to undertake the task. Because of the contribution which progress in the removal of social injustice would make towards the establishment of world peace they included the

[1] An account of these developments in international labour organisation is given in *International Social Progress*, by G. A. Johnston, London, 1924, Chapter II, "The Origins of International Labour Legislation".   [2] Preamble to Part XIII of the Versailles Treaty.

Organisation in the general structure of the League of Nations.

An impartial survey of the work of the Organisation during its first decade shows that remarkable progress has been made. In the compilation of information on labour conditions throughout the world, in the machinery provided for international discussion and cooperation, and in the establishment and application of international Conventions on labour standards the position is incomparably superior to that before the war. Up to the autumn of 1930, little more than a decade from the establishment of the Organisation, thirty-one Draft Conventions had been adopted by the International Labour Conferences, and there had been over four hundred acts of ratification of these Conventions in the different countries. But the survey also indicates the difficulties of the task and the fact which is discussed later that on certain fundamental problems, especially wages, achievements have been meagre.

The difficulties are due to the complication of world economic conditions and the slowness with which fundamental changes in standards of labour conditions can be made. In some countries methods of production are highly efficient, natural resources rich, and labour scarce; in others labour is plentiful, is wastefully used, and natural resources are poor. These cause wide differences in conditions of work, wages, and standards of living. Also habits of consumption and costs of living differ widely from country to country, and these make difficult the comparison of standards of living of the workers in different countries.

Differences in standards of labour conditions are due chiefly to differences in (1) the efficiency of labour; (2) natural resources; (3) the efficiency of capital equipment and industrial organisation in relation to the supply of labour; (4) the extent to which labour is exploited or is free from exploitation. The last of these factors only is responsible for unfair competition. If in one country standards of labour are low owing to low efficiency of labour, poor natural resources or inefficient equipment and organisation, competition is not unfair with other countries which have superior efficiency and resources. This does not, however, imply that international action can contribute to the raising of low labour standards only by the elimination of unfair competition. Low efficiency of labour in some countries may be due either to racial and climatic conditions or to the low standard of living and of working conditions. With racial and climatic differences as with differences in natural resources little or nothing can be done. Experience shows, however, that racial differences have less influence on labour efficiency under modern industrial conditions than is usually supposed, and that the differences in productivity of various races employed on mass production and supplied with equally efficient machinery are not great; the relative efficiencies are much less than present differences in the wage standards of the various races, and these differences would be greatly reduced by a wider distribution of modern capital equipment. But inefficiency due to oppressive conditions of labour and an unduly low standard of living can be gradually remedied. Long hours, bad workshop conditions, and wages so low that food, lodging, and clothing are inadequate leave the worker physically and psychologically incapable of efficient work. But his output can be increased by improving his working conditions and by paying him a more adequate wage. This can be facilitated by international exchange of experience and agreement on improved standards. Such progress would reduce hardship and misery, which is so often a cause of social unrest.

The raising of labour standards reacts not only on the efficiency of the workers but on the efficiency of productive organisation. Where labour is cheap it is often wastefully used, but if the cost of labour is increased organisation and equipment are improved so that the productivity of the worker is raised. The raising of labour standards by international action will therefore tend to reduce the waste of human effort which is so common in backward countries in consequence of lack of efficient equipment and organisation. This will be facilitated by the present tendency for increase in the international mobility of capital.

Improvements in the efficiency of labour and productive organisation in countries which are at present backward will increase rather than diminish the competitive power of these countries. Equilibrium of competitive power between different countries is disturbed if any country increases the severity with which it exploits its labour or improves its productive efficiency. This causes changes in the boundaries of the markets of the various countries. In some areas a country's trade is predominant and strongly established, but at the "frontiers" of its marketing area gains or losses are always taking place according to changes in the relative efficiency of the competing countries. These changes of economic frontiers will not be prevented by international regulation of labour standards. Competition will not be abolished, but its effects on labour standards will be restricted. The object is not to establish a *status quo*, nor necessarily to confer benefits on the advanced countries at the expense of the backward ones; this will result in so far as countries with low standards have been guilty of exploiting their workers. The object is rather to raise the standard of human welfare in all countries, whether by the suppression of exploitation or by increasing the efficiency of labour itself and of the capital equipment and organisation placed at its disposal. Any changes which may result in the relative competitive power of different countries would be based on fairer and more humane conditions of labour. Also, with the coordinated raising of labour standards and of productive efficiency, the backward countries would become better customers than at present for the products of other countries.

By what methods can improvements of labour standards be effected? International action may be attempted either by the establishment of general principles or by the fixing of actual standards. There are certain principles which are capable of universal application, e.g. the right of association and the payment of compensation to victims of industrial accidents. Such principles, based on general ideas of social justice, may be embodied in international conventions or recommendations and applied in all countries.

When, however, attempts are made to establish actual standards, as distinct from principles, the attainment of uniformity is more difficult, and on some questions is quite impracticable. Uniformity may be attained on certain less vital standards. A country may readily agree to prohibit the night work of young persons but hesitate or refuse to establish an eight-hour day for all industrial workers.

Uniformity of standard is not necessary to prevent unfair international competition. On some questions the appropriate method may well be to aim not at uniformity but at somewhat similar advances by all countries. It is true that the authors of Part XIII of the Treaties of Peace looked to uniformity as an ultimate objective, but in practice on the more vital questions, especially hours and wages, allowance for the wide differences in the average standards from one country to another must be made. Thus the Washington Hours Convention lays down a uniform 48-hour week for Western industrial countries, but makes various exceptions, including a 57-hour week in most industries in Japan and a 60-hour week in India. The Conventions fixing the minimum age for admission of children to industrial employment and prohibiting the employment of young persons during the night also make special provisions for India and Japan. This method of making allowance for differences in conditions from one country to another suggests that a similar practice might be adopted also for wages and other problems.

The practice should not, however, be pressed too far. A Convention must represent some progress if it is to be of any value. Merely to embody in a Convention the standards of each country would result in little progress. Yet the representatives, especially of Governments and employers of different countries at the International Labour Conferences, usually endeavour to secure the adoption of standards which conform with the legislation or practice of their own country. They aim at a Convention which calls for no raising of their own standard.

It would, of course, be impracticable to set up standards far in advance of existing practice. Many of the "ideals" of social justice can be attained only gradually. A Convention which is far ahead of present standards in many countries will obtain few ratifications, although it may still be of value by setting a goal towards which progress is directed.[1] Each Convention should, however, represent an advance for some if not for all countries. Often a reasonable method is to embody in a Convention the practice of the more advanced countries, and by pressure of public opinion gradually bring the backward countries up to this level. When this stage is reached the way is prepared for a further step forward; the advanced countries may have shown the direction by having already gone beyond the provisions of the Convention.

Many International Labour Conventions fix minimum standards, but any country which ratifies is quite free to set higher standards. In practice many workers enjoy shorter hours than those fixed by the Washington Eight-Hours Convention; in Great Britain, which has not yet ratified this Convention, the hours of

[1] The Workmen's Compensation Convention is a notable example.

I

labour fixed by collective agreements for large numbers
of workers are less than forty-eight per week. By fixing
only minimum standards rigidity is avoided and progress beyond the minimum can be made in any countries
in which this is warranted by economic conditions. At
the same time the minimum provides a level at which
labour standards are safeguarded against the storms of
international competition.

In considering the various problems of labour conditions, certain ones are of outstanding importance,
namely, hours, wages, and social insurance. Other
subjects, for example, measures for industrial health
and safety and special provisions for the protection of
women, young persons, and children, are also important,
but they are somewhat less fundamental in economic
affairs and especially in international competition.
The International Labour Conference has experienced
little difficulty in reaching agreement on Conventions
prohibiting the night work of women and young
persons, fixing the minimum age for admission of
children to employment in industry, agriculture, or
at sea, and providing for the compulsory medical
examination of children or young persons under
eighteen years of age employed at sea, to ensure that
they are fit for such work. Also, these Conventions,
except that on minimum age for agricultural work,
are amongst those which have received the greatest
number of ratifications. Other Conventions which have
been most widely ratified provide for the establishment of a system of free public employment agencies,
for the payment to seamen of an unemployment
indemnity in the event of the loss or foundering of

their vessels, for granting to agricultural workers the same rights of association as industrial workers, for prohibiting (with certain exceptions) the use of white lead in the internal painting of buildings, for granting a weekly rest of at least twenty-four hours to workers in industrial undertakings, for payment of compensation for incapacity or death caused by occupational diseases, and for granting equal treatment in any country to national and foreign workmen in compensation for industrial accidents.

These Conventions have made an important contribution towards greater uniformity of labour standards in competing countries, especially in Europe. An interesting analysis of ratifications of International Labour Conventions by European countries is given by Mr. H. B. Butler in a paper on "Ten Years' Development of Industrial Standards in Europe", read before the Manchester Statistical Society in March 1930.[1] This shows the considerable progress made, especially in the suppression of child labour and the protection of women and young persons.

Most of these widely ratified Conventions represent accepted humanitarian standards and principles of social justice. As already stated, however, many of them are less fundamental than wages and hours of labour to national and international economic life. Yet less progress has been made in national legislation and international Conventions on wages than on other standards of labour conditions.

[1] Full details of ratifications are given by the Director of the International Labour Office in Annual Reports to the International Labour Conference.

The problems of hours and wages in international competition are discussed below. Special attention is given to wages. It is essential that wages should be regulated by international agreement. Otherwise reduced hours, provision of social insurance benefits, measures for health and safety—all of value for their own sake—might do little to prevent unfair international competition based on unsatisfactory labour conditions. The full force of competition could be concentrated on wages and the advantages from regulation of other conditions could be largely if not altogether withdrawn.

Social insurance, also an important subject, is not separately discussed. Methods of distributing benefits under social insurance schemes are of little importance in international competition. What is important is the cost of the schemes in different countries. For example, according to statistics for the coal-mining industry in 1927, computed by the International Labour Office, employers' social insurance contributions represented an addition to daily wages of 11 to 15 per cent. in Germany (Ruhr), Poland, and Czechoslovakia, but of only 5 per cent. in Great Britain.[1] But for the purposes of international competition contributions to social insurance schemes may be regarded as part of total labour cost. They may therefore be added to wages. Thus, European countries cannot complain of unfair competition from the United States if wages in that country are higher than wages plus social insurance charges in European countries. This does not in any way detract from the importance of developing social

[1] *International Labour Review*, October, 1929.

insurance schemes or withdraw the charge that American workers are not adequately safeguarded against the risks which are covered by social insurance in many other countries. But it does follow for purposes of international competition that social insurance charges may simply be added to wages. Therefore, in comparing wages in different countries in order to determine whether these are unfair or unduly low the amounts contributed for social insurance benefits should be included.[1]

HOURS OF LABOUR

Reference has already been made to the Washington Hours Convention which provides for an eight-hour day and a forty-eight-hour week in industrial undertakings. These conditions were to apply to all Western industrial countries; several exceptions were, however, made, notably for India and Japan. The Convention was passed in 1919, but eleven years later it had been ratified unconditionally by nine countries only; of these only Belgium, Czechoslovakia, and India are of great industrial importance.[2] Five countries had ratified conditionally upon other countries doing so, but as the conditions had not been satisfied they had not applied the Convention. Any considerable progress in the application of the Convention depends on ratification by Great Britain. The ultimate success

---

[1] The wages compared should also include the value of any payments in kind, family allowances, cost of paid holidays, and other pecuniary advantages.
[2] The other countries are Bulgaria, Chile, Greece, Luxemburg, Portugal, and Rumania.

of the Convention, whether in its present or in a slightly amended form, is, however, undoubted. It is economically practicable on the basis of the industrial progress of the last fifty years. Its ratification by all the chief industrial countries will ensure that hours of work in industry are largely shielded from the force of international competition.

The Washington Convention has been supplemented by the Draft Convention, adopted by the International Labour Conference, 1930, which fixes a forty-eight-hour week for salaried workers in commerce and in office work.

The 1930 Conference also discussed a Draft Convention for fixing hours of work of underground workers in coal-mines. The coal-mining industry during recent years has offered the most striking example of the harmful consequences of unregulated competition.[1] The intensity of international competition had resulted in the lengthening of miners' hours and reductions of their wages in various European countries; an outstanding example is the changes in hours and wages in the British coal-mining industry after the 1926 stoppage. The object of the proposed Convention was to fix at a reasonable level the hours of underground miners so that they would henceforth be protected from international competition. There was considerable support in the Conference for the idea that underground miners should have somewhat shorter hours than those fixed by the Washington Convention for other industrial workers. Preliminary agreement

---

[1] See articles in the *International Labour Review*, May 1926, February and June 1928, by Dr. Mack Eastman and M. Fernand Maurette.

was reached that the time spent in the mine should be 7 hours 45 minutes per day (including winding time), and that within three years after the coming into force of the Convention the possibility of a further reduction of hours should be discussed. The Draft Convention failed to secure the necessary two-thirds majority in the Conference. It was agreed, however, that the question should be reconsidered at the 1931 Session, when it is hoped that adequate support will be forthcoming.

Special Conventions providing for shorter hours than those fixed for most classes of industrial workers may be necessary for other industries and occupations besides underground miners. Also, the International Labour Conference has not yet undertaken the difficult task of regulating the hours of work of seamen and of agricultural workers. Further, the Washington Hours Convention does not apply to China, Persia, and Siam; these countries were reserved for future consideration.

The present widely accepted standard of a maximum working week of forty-eight hours for industrial and clerical work is in no sense an absolute standard. It would no doubt be possible to determine by scientific experiments what the *optimum* length of working day should be in each industry, i.e. the duration which would give maximum daily production. The duration would differ for each industry and for the various occupations within each industry. It would also change with the introduction of new processes and methods of work. The fixing of hours of work which differed considerably from one industry to another would, however, be opposed by the workers on social grounds.[1]

Reduction of hours to nine or even eight per day has resulted in an actual increase in daily production in many industries. Excessive hours of labour led to low hourly output; a shortening of the working day has resulted in increase of hourly production, which has more than compensated for the smaller number of hours worked. It is doubtful, however, whether in many occupations this compensation would follow if hours were reduced to less than eight per day. Hourly output would increase, but not enough to compensate for the reduction in the number of hours worked.

It must not be concluded that the eight-hour day is about the limit beyond which reduction of hours should not go. The limit would perhaps be near eight hours if the aim is maximum production. But there is every reason to expect industrial progress to continue in the future and that, in consequence, output per worker will increase. This will provide the basis for a considerable rise in the material standard of living. Material welfare might be greatest from the eight-hour day and the forty-eight-hour week. But the workers would no doubt prefer to enjoy their share of industrial progress partly in higher material standards and partly in increased leisure.

Reductions of hours below the standard set by the Washington Convention depend, therefore, on the rate

[1] For more detailed discussions of this and other aspects of the eight-hour day, see articles in the *International Labour Review*, December 1925, February and August 1926, by Professor Edgar Milhaud and M. Albert Thomas.

of industrial progress and the preference shown by the workers for more leisure instead of maximum material income. Already many workers enjoy shorter hours than the Washington standard. There is a tendency toward a reduction of hours in many industries in advanced countries to forty-five or even less per week. This reduction is becoming steadily more necessary in consequence of the enormous increased capacity of mechanical production.[1] In some industries a five-day week is found to be advantageous, while the system of holidays, often with pay, is growing in importance as a means of affording increased leisure. In several countries legislation providing for paid holidays has been enacted. Developments on these lines will no doubt lead to new international conventions and revision of the Washington Convention so as to consolidate the progress made.

It will not be overlooked that successive reductions in hours of work result in increased overhead charges on industry. These may become especially heavy where costly machinery is installed. The possibility of working two shifts in the day by separate groups of workers is already being discussed, and sometimes practised with the object of saving overhead costs by "sweating" the machinery. Unless this is done the installation of the most efficient machinery may frequently be restricted. Some textile factories claim that it would not be economical to use the most up-to-date automatic looms if they must stand idle

---

[1] During the depression of 1930–31, surplus productive capacity led not only the workers but even a considerable number of employers in the United States to envisage a forty-hour week in the comparatively near future.

for sixteen or more hours of the day. There are evidently social objections to the two-shift system, but it should not prove impossible for these to be overcome especially when the working day is further reduced.

WAGES AND INTERNATIONAL COMPETITION

The wage question is the chief and the most difficult of labour problems, and is intimately related to the whole of economic life. In many industries levels of wages are directly affected by international competition, while business men constantly complain that competitive conditions are unfair because of low-wage standards abroad. In consequence of international competition two problems call for solution : first, to prevent the severity of international competition in any given industry from forcing down the wages of the workers in the industry in different countries to unduly low levels; and, second, to ensure that some countries shall not suffer from unfair competition based on low wages in others.[1]

In the first of these problems the root of the trouble is generally not wages but the over-development of the industry. The industry has more workers and more capital equipment than are required to satisfy the demand for its products. The temptation to seek relief

[1] Unfair competition due to currency depreciation and the consequent fall in real wages and other costs of production in some countries need not now be discussed. It was acute several years ago, and its effects are still felt, but it was a temporary problem the cure for which was currency stability and the gradual restoration of normal wage and price relations within the countries concerned. This situation is now being reached.

by reductions of wages is great, but the advantage
obtained in this way by one country soon leads to
similar measures in others. After all-round reductions
the competitive situation is often left almost unchanged, but wages may have been forced down to
a level which involves privation to the workers. Also,
the process of reduction involves much bitterness both
internationally and between employers and workers
within the different countries.

It is admitted that in some industries the lowering
of costs of production consequent upon wage reductions may lead to increase in demand for the products
and so reduce the intensity of international competition. Where wages in the industry in some or all
countries had previously been high, their reduction
would call for no objection. What is to be avoided
is the forcing down of wages in an over-developed
industry to an unduly low level by successive reductions in different countries. The advantage of any small
increase in demand for the products is outweighed by
the friction involved in securing the wage reductions
and by the harmful consequences of unduly low wages.
In industries producing commodities the demand for
which is inelastic, e.g. coal-mining during recent years,
a lowering of the workers' wage standards leads to
little increase in demand and to little diminution in
the severity of international competition.

For such over-developed industries the solution is
not reduction of wages but transfer of labour and
capital to other industries. Reduction of wages to
unduly low levels in different countries merely diverts
attention from the true remedies and delays their

application. In Chapter III the advantages of international agreements between producers in over-developed industries were indicated. With such agreements each country can determine with considerable accuracy its probable output and the labour force required; the amount of surplus labour in the industry is therefore known and its systematic transfer to other industries can be organised. These agreements could be usefully supplemented by international agreements to maintain at reasonable levels the labour standards, and especially wages, in the industry concerned.

In the circumstances already described, the wage-levels in the different countries may be such that no one country has a competitive advantage over any other, except temporarily during a contest of wage reductions. The severity of international competition and the demand for wage reductions are both consequences of the over-development of the industry. But in the second problem mentioned at the beginning of this section, the difficulties of producers in some countries result from the payment of unfair wages in their industry by producers in one or several other countries. Unless these wages are raised, manufacturers who suffer from this competition will be likely either to demand tariff protection against their foreign competitors or will endeavour to force their own workers to accept lower wages.

Formerly within each country there was much unfair competition because some employers paid sweated wages to their workers, and in consequence other employers found it difficult to maintain reasonable wage standards. In some countries the development of Trade Unionism and the establishment of Trade Boards, or similar systems of wage regulation, have resulted in a considerable diminution, or even complete suppression of sweating. In other countries, however, sweated wages are still paid, and this often involves unfair competition between employers within these countries and in international markets. Among possible remedies is the wider adoption nationally and even internationally of the systems which, in some countries, have resulted in reduction or even elimination of unfair sweated wages.

DISCUSSION OF "UNDULY LOW" AND "UNFAIR" WAGES

Before considering the possibilities of solving these problems it is necessary to discuss the expressions "unduly low" and "unfair" as applied to wages. Unfortunately, both are relative terms; there is no absolute standard by reference to which wages in any given industry may be classified as "unduly low" or "unfair". This increases the difficulties of national and international regulation.

Unduly low wages are usually defined as those which are not sufficient to provide the workers with reasonable subsistence according to prevailing standards. A chief method of determining whether wages in any industry or occupation are unduly low is to compare them for a given *time* unit with the wages paid for work of similar skill in other occupations and industries in the same district or country. This may be supplemented by comparing them with wages at previous dates in the same industry. If workers in one industry receive lower weekly or annual wages than their neighbours of equal skill and experience in most other industries, their standard of living is below the recognised standard of their fellows, and, where the difference is considerable, the result is privation in relation to prevailing habits of consumption.

It is also true that the wage standards of large numbers of workers in some countries are unduly low in relation to standards in other countries. With the progressive development of international trade and mobility of capital, such international differences may gradually diminish. But, both for humanitarian reasons and to improve international relations, the most urgent task is to raise the wages of workers in the lowest paid trades in each country. These are the trades in which the workers are suffering privation in relation to the standards of living of their fellows, and it is also from these unduly low-paid "sweated" trades that the worst forms of unfair international competition are likely to arise.

The question of "unfair wages" demands a more detailed and somewhat theoretical discussion. The expression is widely used without any serious attempt being made to determine whether the use is justified or not. Usually when international competition becomes severe and producers in a particular country are losing markets, they raise the complaint of competition based on unfair wages abroad. Yet the loss of markets may be due either to a decline in their own efficiency of productive organisation and equipment or to an increase in this efficiency in foreign countries.

It has already been indicated that wages may be unduly low from the workers' point of view without being unfair between different employers either within a country or internationally. If all employers in an industry are paying unduly low wages, there may be no question of some employers having a competitive advantage in wages over their rivals; the competition may be "fair" between employers, although the earnings of the workers may be so low as to involve them and their families in misery and privation.

From the point of view of international competition the wages paid to workers in one country are fair in relation to those paid in another if the ratio between the wages income of the two groups of workers is equal to the ratio between their efficiencies.[1] In considering whether international competition based on low wages is unfair, it is therefore essential to examine not merely the wages paid to the workers but also the standards of efficiency. It is necessary, further, to examine the efficiency of productive methods in the different countries. If this is done it is frequently found that international differences are much greater in wages than in labour costs. This may be illustrated by the relation between wages and labour costs in cotton-spinning in Japan, England, and the United States. According to data compiled by Professor Orchard, wages in South Carolina are four times, and in England three times, those in Japan. But the

[1] Cf. a discussion of fair and unfair wages and of methods for their statistical determination, by Professor A. C. Pigou, in *Economic of Welfare*, Part III, Chapters XIV and XV.

American worker, with the equipment and organisation furnished him, is nearly three times as efficient as the Japanese worker, and labour costs per pound of yarn are only about one-third greater in America than in Japan. The margin between European and Japanese costs is even less.[1] Often low-paid labour is so inefficient and wastefully used that labour cost per unit of output is relatively high. On the other hand, workers in receipt of high wages per hour, per week, or other period of time, may have such a high rate of production that the cost per unit of output is low.

Lower labour costs in some countries than in others are frequently a consequence more of superior natural resources and of greater efficiency of capital equipment and organisation available for the worker than of the higher efficiency of labour. There is, however, a tendency in modern industry, with mass production and standardisation of product, for machinery and methods of manufacture to become more similar in different countries. Manufacturers are in closer contact than ever before, and machinery and methods which give good results in one country are soon introduced in another. For example, British textile machinery is exported to Japan, India, China, and other countries, and provides a basis for similarity of productive conditions. The development of international companies with manufacturing establishments in different countries results in the wide application of similar methods

[1] The *Geographical Review* published by the American Geographical Society of New York, April 1929, article by John E. Orchard, pp. 196–7. Professor Orchard points out that Japanese labour costs are further increased by cost of recruitment, cost of dormitories, and bonuses paid upon discharge.

of production and uniformity of product. The position
in the different works of the Ford Motor Company
may be taken as an example. The Chairman of the
Company (Sir Percival Perry), in his speech at the first
Ordinary General Meeting of the Company in March
1930, stated that "the uniformity of the product of
the Company affords an almost unique opportunity
to make international comparisons. Similar tools and
machinery and the same methods of manufacturing
and assembly are employed in every Ford factory
throughout the world. The Company and its associated
companies employ on almost identical work English-
men, Irishmen, Dutchmen, Frenchmen, Danes, Ger-
mans, Italians, Spaniards, Swedes, Finns, and Turks.
Comparative statistics have enabled us to establish the
fact that the American worker is no miracle-monger.
Neither is the British, Irish, or continental artisan an
inferior creature. Given like conditions and treatment,
our workers here in Europe actually beat their American cousins, as proved by the standard of our minute
costs."

Clearly where conditions of production are the same
and labour is equally efficient, wages should be equal
if they are to be fair in relation to international trade.
The position in factories of the Ford Motor Company
may be taken as an illustration, but the conclusions
would apply equally to separate companies in competition against one another. If the Ford "chain" is
running as fast in Dagenham or Manchester as in
Detroit, and if the British workers can maintain the
pace, they should be paid at the same money rate as
workers in Detroit. Actually the Ford Company plans

K

to pay to its European workers a wage which will have a purchasing power equivalent to that of the wage paid in Detroit.[1] As the cost of living is lower in European cities than in Detroit, this implies the payment of a money wage lower than that in Detroit. It would give the workers in the different countries similar quantities of food, clothing, housing accommodation, and other commodities and would thus provide a similar material basis for physical efficiency. The Ford Company are evidently of the opinion that if the European worker is as well fed, housed, and clothed as the American worker, his productive efficiency will be the same. They therefore intend to pay wages which will supply these requirements for physical efficiency.

These wages, though higher than the general levels of wages now being paid in European countries on the basis of demand and supply, and though fair to the workers by giving them the same standard of living, would be unfair for international trade. The money wage for equal efficiency being lower in Europe than in Detroit, the labour cost of producing cars in Europe would be less than that in Detroit. This would give the European establishments an advantage over the one in Detroit.[2] This would be equally true if the European and American establishments were in com-

[1] At the request of the Ford Motor Company the International Labour Office is conducting an enquiry to determine the cost in the various European cities of the commodities which the Detroit worker can purchase with a wage of seven dollars a day.
[2] If, however, the American establishment is better located for marketing cars with little expense, and can sell them at a higher price, it has greater capacity to pay, and in consequence the workers would be likely to secure higher remuneration.

petition with one another instead of being in the same organisation.[1] It cannot, however, be concluded that the "unfair" relation demands a raising of the European money wage to the Detroit level. "Fairness" is merely a relative term, and it would be equally reasonable to claim that wages in Detroit were too high as that wages in Europe were too low. As already indicated there is no absolute test of what is a fair wage; only by taking account of the conditions of demand for and supply of labour in the different countries can any approximation be made of what level is practicable.

However, the present levels of wages in different countries show wider differences than would be warranted if standardised modern methods of manufacture were more widely employed. American workers receive wages three times as high as workers in some of the countries of Central and Southern Europe, not because as workers they are three times as efficient, but because they are supplied with better machinery and organisation. Often the labour required by modern industry is largely unskilled or semi-skilled. Working under similar conditions this labour in different countries would not be likely to show very wide differences in efficiency. With international mobility of capital, the more general adoption of similar methods of manufacture in different countries and progress in

[1] In the Ford establishments the European workers in a sense compete against the Detroit workers at least for the European market even if no cars produced in Europe are sold in the United States. Actually Ford tractors manufactured at Cork are being imported into the United States and compete with tractors produced by American companies.

transportation, the present relative levels of wages are likely to be profoundly modified. The movement of capital itself will be determined in part at least by wage-levels and relative labour efficiency in different countries.

If in different countries methods of production are similar but efficiencies of labour differ, wages would be fair if in the same ratio as the efficiencies. If Lancashire cotton weavers operate four looms and Indian cotton weavers with similar looms working at the same speed and producing similar cloth operate only one loom, wages are fair if the Lancashire weaver's wage is four times that paid to the Indian weaver.[1]

The most usual situation, however, still is that methods of manufacture and natural resources are different from one country to another. Where superior natural resources or higher efficiency of productive methods are responsible for lower labour costs the charge of unfair competition is not justified. Lower labour costs based on extraction of coal from a richer seam could not be considered unfair. Similarly, an inefficient firm or industry in one country can hardly make a complaint merely because a firm or industry abroad is more efficient. Its first step is to put its own house in order.[2] No action should be taken either nationally or internationally which would penalise the employment of the best methods or the utilisation

[1] The Lancashire worker might indeed receive somewhat more than four times the Indian's wage as he would involve lower overhead charges.
[2] It is necessary for an industry to be reasonably efficient before it is accorded protection against unfair foreign competition under the British Safeguarding of Industries Act.

of the richest resources. Again, if work is done under different conditions of production, the comparative efficiency of workpeople is not measured by their relative outputs, and, therefore, in order that wages may be fair, rates per unit of output should be so adjusted that different outputs representing equal efficiencies shall receive a similar reward.

Various situations may be illustrated. Thus, American business men often claim that productive efficiency in very many industries in the United States is so high that labour costs per unit of output are the lowest in the world, and then they will go on to demand higher protective tariffs as a safeguard against goods produced by workers with lower wage standards abroad! Similar arguments are not unknown in other countries. Comparisons are frequently made between hourly or weekly wages in Britain and in continental European and Far Eastern countries by converting the wages paid abroad into sterling by the rates of exchange. If the foreign wage-levels prove to be considerably below the British level, British employers tend immediately to conclude that competition is unfair without seriously enquiring into relative efficiencies. On the other hand, it would be difficult for countries with high labour costs but low hourly, weekly, or annual wages to complain that they suffer from the unfair competition of countries with lower labour costs but higher wages based on superior efficiency. But although this is generally true, there may be certain exceptions; thus competition would be unfair if in one country workers received somewhat higher real wages than in another, but attained considerably lower labour costs by being worked at excessive speed or for excessive hours.

The complaint of unfairness is more reasonable where competition is based on lower labour costs and where also the workers receive lower hourly, weekly, or annual wages. These joint conditions—lower labour costs and lower real wages—often justify the charge of unfair competition. Where wages on a time basis are very much lower in one country than in another and the industrial development of the two countries is fairly similar, there is strong presumption of unfair competition.[1] Thus statistics of real wages published by the International Labour Office show that in several countries of continental Europe real wages are 20 per cent. or even 30 or 40 per cent. below the British level.[2] But in many of the industries in these countries a rapid process of rationalisation has recently been applied, and it seems fairly certain that, by these industrial developments and the maintenance of low wages, labour costs have fallen in relation to those in

[1] Cf. Board of Trade, Safeguarding of Industries *Report of the Woollen and Worsted Committee*, Cmd. 3355, London, 1929, pages 20 and 21. The Committee in examining evidence of low wages in foreign countries were of the opinion that "the only way in which inferior conditions of the employment of labour could give rise to 'unfair competition' is by unduly depressing the wages cost per unit of product of the foreign goods which come into competition with British manufacturers". They considered, however, that where conditions of labour were substantially inferior abroad, there was a presumption that labour costs would also be lower. The Committee evidently had in mind particularly conditions in France where, according to the data available, wages were only one-half to two-thirds of the Yorkshire level; they found it "quite impossible to believe that any difference of efficiency between the labour of the two countries could be sufficient to counterbalance the great inferiority in earnings".   [2] See tables on pages 156–157 and 159.

Britain. The consequence is increased pressure of foreign competition and loss of markets by British producers. British employers cannot reasonably make the charge of unfairness because industry in France, Belgium, and Czechoslovakia has become relatively more efficient. But they may well complain that, owing to the effect of customary standards, wages in these countries have not risen as much as would be warranted by the rise in efficiency.

To summarise, it has been indicated that the expressions "unduly low wages" and "unfair wages" are both relative; neither is capable of absolute definition. Unduly low wages are generally regarded as those which involve hardship and privation to the worker and his family in relation to the prevalent standard of living among workers' families. Unduly low wages are often also unfair, and there is urgent need for each country to raise the wage standards of its lowest paid workers more nearly to the general level. In international competition there is a strong presumption that wages are unfair if in any industry they are considerably lower in one country than in another, and if labour costs per unit of output are also lower.

In concluding this section emphasis may be laid on the importance of adequate statistics as a basis for international regulation of wages. The above discussion has shown the need for comparable information on wages in the various industries and occupations in different countries. Many statistics are available on hourly or weekly wages although they are still far from comparable internationally. But on labour costs per unit of output practically no reliable figures exist, and there is no adequate basis for determining whether wages in any two countries are fair or not. Statistics on labour costs are occasionally published but are so meagre that they permit of only the most tentative conclusions.[1] The International Labour Office has begun to make international comparisons of wages, but for many industries no comparable information is available. Also proposals for enquiries into labour costs, e.g. in the cotton and wool textile industries, have encountered so much opposition that they have had to be abandoned. In some countries the employers still regard statistics of wages and labour costs as secrets of production!

Each country should compile information showing the wages in its lowest paid trades in comparison with the general level in the chief industries. It was the publication of such information in Great Britain before the war which led to the anti-sweating campaign, the passing of the Trade Boards Acts, and the gradual elimination of the worst forms of sweating. The International Labour Office might give special attention to industries suffering from severe international competition. It has already compiled information on wages and labour costs in the coal-mining industry and is planning an enquiry into wages in the textile industry.

It would be especially valuable if information could be compiled to show the wages, labour costs, and the

[1] For example, relative labour and total costs in cotton weaving in a mill in Lancashire and a mill in Japan, compiled by John H. Grey of Burnley, are published in the *Transactions of the Manchester Statistical Society, Session 1927-1928*, p. 45.

See also "Time and Labor Cost of Production in the Woolen and Worsted Industry, United States, England, France, Germany", published in the *Monthly Labor Review* of the United States Bureau of Labor Statistics, September 1928.

labour efficiency of workers employed under similar conditions of production in the different countries. Comparisons could most readily be made by international trusts with factories in different countries, e.g. the Ford Motor Company, the Swedish Match Corporation, the British American Tobacco Company, and the American Radiator Company. Comparisons could, however, be made also by the selection in different countries of establishments in which similar machinery and methods are employed and which manufacture similar products.

Information on these lines would provide the basis for improvements both by national action and by international agreement. The publication of international comparisons showing wages in some countries to be considerably below the levels in neighbouring countries has already led to demands for improvement both by the workers themselves and by public opinion. Also, effective international regulation largely depends on the development of an adequate basis of statistical information.

INTERNATIONAL REGULATION OF WAGES

The necessity for international regulation of wages, as well as of other conditions of labour, has already been indicated. The objects are chiefly to prevent for humanitarian reasons the payment of unduly low wages, to provide a stimulus to the more efficient use of labour, and to prevent unfair international competition. The attainment of these objects would ensure that improvements in hours and other conditions of labour would not be made at the expense of wages. It would remove causes of social unrest and lead to improvement in industrial and international relations.

International agreement may be reached either on actual wage standards or on principles to be observed in the different countries. There are greater difficulties in securing agreement upon standards than upon principles. Principles, if kept general enough, are often readily accepted; for example, the signatories of the Peace Treaties agreed to the principle of paying an adequate living wage as this is understood in the time and country. But the difficulty of interpretation arises when the attempt is made to convert such a principle into a standard. Principles alone are not enough; they must be completed by agreement on actual standards.

For fixing wage standards by international agreement, a method different from that adopted in the Washington Hours Convention and other Conventions of the International Labour Organisation seems essential. The Washington Hours Convention, for example, aimed at fixing the same standard of hours for workers in all manufacturing industries in all countries. The exceptions made for Japan and India were regarded rather as temporary transitional measures. An examination of the wage statistics available for different industries in different countries gives convincing proof of the impossibility of securing agreement on international uniformity. Statistics show that time wages in some countries are double or even treble those in others, and fundamental changes in economic conditions would be necessary before anything approaching equality could be attained. Such changes are not likely to be effected in the early future.

A scale which would afford some protection against unduly low wages of workers in countries where levels are relatively high would be quite beyond the capacity of countries in which the average standard is considerably lower. On the other hand a minimum scale, which would be of real value in countries where wages are relatively low, would be so much below the average level in countries with higher standards as to afford no adequate safeguard against underpayment.

Differences in the wage-levels in some of the chief countries are illustrated by the figures tabulated below, based on statistics compiled by the International Labour Office. The money-wage figures are averages calculated from the wages of workers in about thirty occupations in the building, engineering, furniture-making, food, and printing industries, and in electrical installation, electric power distribution, transport, and municipal service. The index numbers of real wages represent the relative purchasing power of the money wages over commodities of ordinary consumption, chiefly food, fuel, and light. The figures are subject to various reservations, and more complete information would give somewhat different results.[1] They are, however, adequate to show the wide differences in wage-levels from one country to another.

[1] The methods used are described and the reservations indicated in the *International Labour Review*, especially the number for October 1924. See also a paper on the subject read by the author before the Royal Statistical Society in April 1930, *Journal of the Royal Statistical Society*, Vol. XCIII, Part III, 1930; the table is reproduced from this paper.

AVERAGE HOURLY WAGES IN NATIONAL CURRENCIES AND IN DOLLARS, WITH INDEX NUMBERS, AND INDEX NUMBERS OF REAL WAGES OF ADULT MALE WORKERS IN CERTAIN OCCUPATIONS IN DIFFERENT COUNTRIES, JANUARY 1930[1]

Country	Number of Towns	Average Hourly Wage		Index Numbers of Average Hourly Wage In Dollars (Great Britain = 100)	Index Numbers of Real Wages	
		In National Currency	In Dollars		Based on Cost of Food	Based on Cost of Food, Fuel, Light, and Soap
			I. Time Rates of Wage			
Australia	2	2s. 5d.	0.59	174	152	148
Austria[2]	3	1.28 Sch.	0.18	53	53	52
Canada	6	0.70 $	0.70	206	168	165
France[3]	4	5.00 Fr.	0.19	56	61	59
Germany	6	1.17 R.M.	0.28	82	77	77
Great Britain	7	1s. 5d.	0.34	100	100	100
Irish Free State	3	1s. 6d.	0.36	106	100	97
Italy	7	3.31 L.	0.17	50	51	—
Netherlands	4	0.72 Fl.	0.29	85	89	87
Spain	4	1.21 Pts.	0.17	50	49	—
United States	10	0.89 $	0.89	262	197[4]	197[4]

II. *Time and Piece Earnings*

Czechoslovakia[5] ..	3	7.54 Kr.	0.22	61	73	70
Denmark ..	1	1.56 Kr.	0.42	117	107	107
Esthonia ..	2	0.41 E.Kr.	0.11	31	43	43
Germany[6] ..	6	1.25 R.M.	0.30	83	78	78
Great Britain[7] ..	7	1s. 5¾d.	0.36	100	100	100
Poland ..	4	1.55 Zl.	0.18	50	65	62
Sweden ..	3	1.54 Kr.	0.41	114	109	108

[1] As indicated in the text, different results would be shown if the statistics covered a greater number of industries and occupations, if weekly or annual wages were taken instead of hourly wages, and if the unit used in calculating the real wages indices included also clothing and shelter.

[2] Minimum rates.

[3] The wage includes an estimated supplement of 2 per cent. for family allowances.

[4] Indices of about 160 would probably be more representative of the *general* level of wages of adult male workers in the chief manufacturing industries, and 150 for unskilled adult male workers; the figures would be lower still if allowance were made for high rents in the U.S.A. The Canadian indices would also be lower for similar reasons.

[5] For workers 25 to 40 years of age; allowance for paid holidays included.

[6] Estimated earnings 7 per cent. above average rate.

[7] Estimated earnings 5 per cent. above average rate.

International differences in wage-levels and also in labour costs are illustrated by the figures given opposite for the coal-mining industry. They are based on data compiled by the International Labour Office for the year 1927; they cover all workers, underground and surface, and include the value of payments in kind, and the contributions of employers and workers to social insurance schemes.[1]

The differences between comparative labour costs of production, comparative hourly or weekly money wages, comparative real wages, together with differences in habits of consumption, classification of workers, methods of work, methods of wage payment, and in the importance of social insurance charges render extremely complicated the task of international wage regulation. This was clearly revealed by the investigations and discussions of the International Labour Organisation when recently considering the possibilities of an international agreement on wages in the coal-mining industry.

In view of the wide wage differences from one industry to another, as well as from one country to another, it is essential that in international measures for fixing wage standards each industry should be considered separately. This conclusion might indeed be reached from a study of collective agreements fixing wage rates in different countries. Almost always agreements are limited to a single industry, or even to certain occupations within an industry. It is true that in Australia and New Zealand basic or minimum wages are fixed which apply to a large number of industries, but this is exceptional. It is evident that

---

[1] *International Labour Review*, October 1929.

AVERAGE DAILY EARNINGS AND WAGES COST PER TON OF COAL, WITH INDEX NUMBERS IN THE CHIEF COAL-PRODUCING COUNTRIES OF EUROPE IN 1927

| Country | Average Daily Earnings | | | | Average Wages Cost per Metric Ton of Commercially Disposable Coal | | |
| | In National Currency | In Gold Francs | Index Numbers (Great Britain = 100) | | In National Currency | In Gold Francs | Index Numbers of Cost in Gold Francs (Great Britain = 100) |
			Of Earnings in Gold Francs	Of Purchasing Power of Earnings			
Germany (Ruhr) ..	9.90 R.M.	12.18	84	80	9.11 R.M.	11.21	78
Belgium	46.64 Fr.	6.73	47	68	102.80 Fr.	14.85	104
France	38.65 Fr.	7.86	54	66[2]	71.13 Fr.	14.47	101
Great Britain ..	11s. 6d.	14.46	100	100	11s. 4d.	14.29	100
Netherlands ..	5.87 Fl.	12.19	84	100	6.18 Fl.	12.83	90
Poland (Upper Silesia)	10.29 Zl.	6.03	42	54	8.29 Zl.	4.86	34
Saar	44.13 Fr.[1]	8.97[1]	63[1]	69[1]	69.97 Fr.	14.23	100
Czechoslovakia ..	52.50 Kr.	8.05	56	67	61.43 Kr.	9.42	66

[1] Per man-shift. [2] Nord and Pas-de-Calais.

international regulation must start with particular industries.

International agreement on wage standards might be established by different types of machinery. It would not be impossible for the method of collective agreements to be extended into the international field. In several countries agreements are now nation-wide in their application. The obstacles in the way of extending agreements so as to cover neighbouring countries should not prove insuperable. For its greatest success this development would demand a high degree of organisation of employers and workers in each country as this would ensure that an agreement in any industry would be observed by all, or almost all, establishments within the countries concerned. The reaching of international collective agreements on wage rates may be facilitated by the growth of international cartels, of companies with establishments in several countries, and of international trade union organisations.

A development of the idea of fixing wages internationally by collective agreement would be for international machinery to be set up in order to regulate wages in any given industry. The machinery might be set up for the sole purpose of fixing wages. Alternatively wages might be fixed by a body set up for other purposes. If, for example, an international coal organisation were set up to regulate production or markets, and for other economic purposes, it might also undertake to regulate wages. Such an organisation might be representative not only of employers and workers but also of the consumers. For wage-fixing purposes it would be a kind of international trade board. The work of such an organisation would no doubt be closely associated with the International Labour Organisation on similar lines to the Joint Maritime Board.

Another method of fixing wage standards internationally would be through the machinery of the International Labour Organisation. A procedure similar to that adopted with a view to the regulation of hours of labour in the coal-mining industry would be suitable. For this industry a considerable amount of preliminary discussion and statistical investigation was undertaken. A Technical Conference was then held to consider the main lines of agreement, and a draft agreement was submitted to the International Labour Conference. It must be noted that the application of this method would imply that wages would have to be controlled by Governments far more than at present, and a very real difficulty arises because the great majority of Governments are still unwilling to undertake wide responsibility for wage regulation.

It would therefore be impracticable to undertake simultaneously a regulation of wages in a large number of industries, nor is this perhaps necessary or desirable. Special attention might be given to industries which are suffering from severe international competition, or where complaints have been raised that competition from certain countries is unfair owing to unduly low wages, and Governments, in association with employers and workers, might agree to apply conventions regulating wages in such industries. As already stated, the International Labour Office has undertaken enquiries

L

into the wages in the coal-mining industry and is making preparation for an enquiry into the wages and other conditions of labour in the cotton and wool textile industries.

Several different types of agreement would be possible. It has been already indicated that an international minimum wage scale for fixing equal rates in all countries would be generally impracticable. The simplest kind of international agreement would be a form of wage truce. This might be useful for preventing wages in an over-developed industry from being forced down to an unduly low level by pressure of international competition. A wage truce would avoid the successive reductions of wages in different countries which often involve industrial conflict and leave the relative competitive situation largely unchanged. An agreement might be reached in an over-developed industry that no reduction would be made for an agreed period; for example, for a year or two years, after which the situation would be reviewed internationally on the basis of the changed economic conditions. There would be difficulty in securing such an agreement if some countries had already secured a competitive advantage by reductions in wages. This difficulty might be overcome on the basis of statistical investigations by providing a wage truce for most countries, with an undertaking by other countries to raise their wages by an agreed percentage within a specified period.

A second type of international minimum wage scale could be established by relating the wages in any industry in different countries according to an agreed ratio. Thus the wages of a selected category of workers might be represented by an index of 100 in Great Britain, by an index of 85 in Germany, an index of 75 in Czechoslovakia, and so on. Wages in the different countries would be fixed in accordance with the agreed indices. This system is similar to that applied in certain countries in national collective agreements which fix wages in different districts according to agreed ratios. Thus in Great Britain wages in the building industry were ascertained in various towns, and the towns graded, and the wages in the different grades of towns are related to one another in accordance with an established scale. This system has been applied in other industries in this country, and is extensively used in Germany and in certain other countries. The ratios for the various districts are usually based at first on existing levels of wages, but other factors, including differences in the cost of living and changes in the economic conditions, are considered. An international wage scale established on these principles would provide for the adjustment of wages in different occupations and districts.

Agreements providing for a ratio scale would necessarily involve the establishment of an agreed ratio, and it is admitted that this would involve both statistical and political difficulties. Another type of international agreement might, however, be reached which would make full allowance for differences in wages in any industry in the different countries by relating wages in the industry in each country to the country's own *general* level of wages. It might be agreed internationally that wages in a particular industry should not be allowed to fall below a certain percentage of the average level of wages in the chief industries of the country. For example, Governments might undertake that hourly wages of workers in any industry should not fall below 90 per cent. of the general average hourly wage. The international agreement, in addition to specifying the percentage, would lay down methods by which the average wage should be calculated and the industries to be included in the average. These industries might vary from country to country in accordance with the relative importance of the different industries in the national life.

It was stated earlier that international agreements on wages might deal either with standards or with principles. Principles may be either general or appropriate to particular industries. The International Labour Conference has already adopted a Convention on minimum wage-fixing machinery which embodies a general principle. This principle is recognition by Governments of an obligation to prevent the payment of exceptionally low wages. States which ratify the Convention undertake to establish machinery for fixing wages in trades where there are no methods for effective wage regulation, and where wages are exceptionally low. The Convention is very elastic as it leaves to the individual Governments the decision as to what they consider to be exceptionally low wages. Also they are free to decide not to fix wages in a particular trade, even though it is agreed that wages are exceptionally low and there are no methods for their effective regulation. It is hoped that pressure of public opinion within the different countries will ensure the adoption of a reasonable definition of exceptionally low wages and the application of the machinery in all branches of industry in which on enquiry wages are found to be exceptionally low. Up to the present, however, several countries which have ratified the Convention are applying it only to a small number of workers, chiefly in the home-working trades. This is the position in Germany and France where the legislation in force does little, if anything, to protect factory workers. In Great Britain, on the other hand, minimum wage-fixing machinery under the Trade Boards Acts is applied more extensively, and covers over a million and a quarter workers in factories and workshops in about forty different branches of industry. A system of wage regulation is also in force in Great Britain for agricultural workers under the Agricultural Wages (Regulation) Act, 1924.

If, after several years, experience shows that the Convention on Minimum Wage-Fixing Machinery is very differently applied in various countries, it would seem necessary to attempt the establishment of a stronger Convention by which Governments would undertake to fix minimum wages in all unduly low-paid unorganised trades. To secure reasonable uniformity of application the Convention might include a definition of "unduly low wages". Alternatively, the task of developing uniformity of application might be undertaken by an international commission.

In addition to recognition of the general principle of preventing payment of unduly low wages, certain special principles might be agreed upon for particular industries. The international adoption of principles which had worked satisfactorily in some countries would be of value. Thus in some countries, e.g. in

Great Britain in the coal-mining and iron and steel industries, wages are regulated in relation to net proceeds or to changes in the price of the product. The underlying idea here is to relate wages to some factor which varies with the prosperity of the industry, i.e. in proportion to its capacity to pay. An international study of these and other principles would be of value in developing methods by which wages could be adjusted without unnecessary friction, and might lead to improvement of industrial relations within the different countries. An extension of the application of these principles might also provide a basis for international coordination of wage policy and methods of regulation.[1]

It is recognised that many of the suggestions outlined above can be adopted only slowly and that they will demand a long process of development. This will include the evolution of machinery for international wage negotiations in different industries, of principles suitable for application in different countries, and of the statistics necessary on time rates and earnings and also on labour costs, if actual international wage scales are to be fixed.

[1] An international study of principles and methods of wage regulation in the coal-mining industry has been undertaken by the International Labour Office.

CHAPTER VII

MONETARY STABILITY

International conflict in monetary policy is more subtle in its operation but no less harmful in its effects than tariff walls, cut-throat competition for markets and conflict in labour standards. In fact, it is sometimes the underlying source from which these other struggles spring. The various countries are so closely related through international trade and the foreign exchanges that isolated national action in the monetary field produces harmful consequences abroad. Only by international cooperation can a satisfactory monetary system be evolved.

A chief use of money is to provide a standard of value—a medium in which the values of commodities and services may be expressed. For this purpose stability of value is of first importance for money as it is for weights, measures, and other standards. If the future value of money is uncertain, additional risk is involved in undertaking contracts expressed in money, while unfortunate social and industrial consequences may result from unforeseen changes in its value. Yet up to the present the world has endured the vagaries of widely fluctuating money values. Until recently, this might be excused because of inadequate knowledge of the factors operating, ignorance of methods, and absence of machinery for effecting stability. It was even thought that monetary value could not be controlled. Now, however, such excuses are not valid. In banking and financial circles at least the factors operating and

methods of securing greater monetary stability are well
known, while control could be effected either through
machinery which already exists or which could readily
be established.

Historical reviews show remarkable changes through
the centuries in monetary values with a general long-
period process of depreciation.[1] The commodities used
as basis for the monetary system have been repeatedly
changed, the most recent being the gradual adoption
by the chief countries of gold instead of silver.

Experience during the greater part of the nineteenth
century in the use of gold as basis of the monetary
system had indeed shown a long-period stability in its
value. Thus, as Mr. Keynes points out, the purchasing
power of money over commodities was approximately
the same in or about the years 1826, 1841, 1855,
1862, 1867, 1871, and 1915. Purchasing power was
also similar in the years 1844, 1881, and 1914, and,
taking the price index during these years as 100, the
maximum fluctuation in either direction for the period
of close on a century from 1826 to the outbreak of
war was 30 points, the index never rising above 130
and never falling below 70. "No wonder that we came
to believe in the stability of money contracts over a
long period. The metal gold might not possess all the
theoretical advantages of an artificially regulated
standard, but it could not be tampered with and had
proved reliable in practice."[2]

Even the relatively small variations in the value

[1] Cf. J. M. Keynes, *A Tract on Monetary Reform*, London, 1923;
see also *A Treatise on Money*, London, 1930.
[2] *Ibid.*, p. 11.

of gold during almost a century preceding the war showed that the gold standard was imperfect. Such imperfections, though attended by social and industrial disadvantages which will be examined later, might be tolerated if there was any certainty that a similar degree of stability would be maintained in the future. But there is no reason to believe that the circumstances which contributed to maintain fair stability of gold value before the war will continue in the future. The real value of gold is determined very similarly to that of any other commodity by the law of supply and demand, although demand is somewhat artificial. The supply of gold available for monetary purposes consists of existing stocks together with new supplies from the mines less the amounts used in the arts, e.g. for jewellery and other commodities. Demand depends mainly on the volume of goods and services exchanged in currencies based on gold. An increase in population and progress in the production of commodities and in trade will increase the demand for gold. The adoption of the gold standard by more countries and increase in the gold reserves of any country also increase the demand for gold. On the other hand, there are various methods of economising gold including increase in the use of cheques, abandonment of the use of gold coin, and diminution in the relation of gold reserves to the volume of currency.

During the nineteenth century the demand for gold steadily increased owing to increase in the volume of transactions. Certain measures of economy in the use of gold were introduced, but there would have been a considerable appreciation in its value, i.e. a fall in the general level of prices of other commodities and services, if important discoveries of gold-mines had not been made. Thus there was appreciation of gold and a generally declining trend of commodity prices during the second quarter of the nineteenth century, but these trends were reversed about the middle of the century, largely in consequence of the great increase in gold production which followed the important discoveries in California and Australia. Commodity prices continued to rise and the value of gold to fall until 1873, but subsequently for more than twenty years the trend was again reversed, the cause being mainly increased demand for gold, especially by Germany, which adopted gold as basis for her currency, and by the United States of America. A rise in the output of gold, including that of the newly discovered Klondyke and South African mines, was in part responsible for the rise in commodity prices and fall in the value of gold from 1896 to the outbreak of war. These various discoveries of gold contributed largely to the maintenance of an exceptional degree of long-period monetary stability before the war.[1]

There is every reason to believe that world economic progress and increase in the volume of production and therefore of goods and services exchanged will continue in the future. Clearly, therefore, an increase in the supply of money will be necessary if a continuous fall in commodity prices is to be avoided. It seems certain also that the gold standard in some form will long be

---

[1] A detailed survey of the movements of prices during the period 1820–1914 in relation to the economic and monetary factors underlying these movements is given by Mr. (now Sir) W. T. Layton in *An Introduction to the Study of Prices*, London, 1920.

retained. In these circumstances monetary stability
can only be attained by the growth of gold reserves
in proportion to the increase of production and trade
or by international cooperation to adjust the monetary
demand for gold to the supply available.

But it is improbable that the production of the mines
will keep pace with the increasing world demand for
gold. Some experts, it is true, refer to improved methods
of extraction which will enable gold to be produced
in considerable quantities from ores which hitherto
have been unprofitable. But there is now wide agreement among experts that a world shortage of gold
is inevitable. The Gold Delegation appointed by the
Financial Committee of the League of Nations reported
in September 1930 that "the evidence points, in our
opinion, conclusively to the prospect of a serious
situation arising as soon as, or shortly after, business
activity revives, unless steps to alleviate it are taken
in time. Moreover, unless new and unexpected sources
of supply are discovered, the decline in the output of
gold is likely to continue at an accelerated rate after
1940, as the South African Mines, which account for
over 50 per cent. of present annual production, become
gradually exhausted. . . . That situation will, of course,
be further aggravated if countries endeavour once
more to put gold coin into circulation, or if the tendency, which has been noticeable in certain quarters,
to convert foreign asset reserves into gold is accentuated".[1] If, therefore, world economic progress is not

[1] *Interim Report of the Gold Delegation of the Financial Committee,*
League of Nations, C. 375, M. 161. 1930. 11, Geneva, September 8,
1930, page 17. Professor Gustav Cassel has repeatedly called attention during the last decade to this danger and to the importance

to be hampered by a long period of declining price-levels, international cooperation is necessary to prevent the harmful consequences of a scarcity of gold and of isolated national action in monetary policy.

The need for international cooperation to maintain monetary stability is not, however, dependent on accepting the view that the world is now facing a shortage of gold with a long period of falling commodity prices. It is practically certain that an unregulated gold standard will result in monetary instability whether through a continuous shortage of gold, a continuous surplus with rising commodity prices, or alternations of shortage and surplus with successive declines and rises in the commodity price-level. Only by world cooperation in adjusting demand to the supply of monetary gold can stability be ensured.

ECONOMIC AND SOCIAL CONSEQUENCES OF INSTABILITY[1]

Before considering methods of securing monetary stability, a brief sketch may be given of the economic and social consequences of instability. These will be examined as they affect the business world, the wage and salary earner, and the investor. The results of shortage of gold and falling commodity prices may be reviewed first, as the world is now experiencing this

of international cooperation to prevent harmful consequences; see his *Memorandum on the World's Monetary Problems* submitted to the International Financial Conference, Brussels, 1920, pp. 36-7. His conclusions are supported by those of an increasing number of investigators. See, for example, the evidence of Mr. Joseph Kitchin before the Royal Commission on Indian Currency and Finance.

[1] Cf. J. M. Keynes, *A Tract on Monetary Reform*, London, 1923, and J. R. Bellerby, *Monetary Stability*, London, 1925.

form of instability and will probably continue to do so unless remedial measures by international cooperation are taken.

The declining level of commodity prices due to scarcity of gold tends to reduce the profitableness of production and thus to cause industrial depression and unemployment. This is in part because the real burden of fixed charges on industry increases as prices fall. Thus fixed interest rates paid by an undertaking on capital and other borrowed money have a higher purchasing power after a fall in prices than when the capital was raised or the loans contracted. Rent and rate charges tend to lag behind the fall in prices, and their real cost therefore increases. Buildings and machinery, stocks of finished goods and materials in process of manufacture—all decline in value as prices fall. Also the business man is called upon to contribute his share of taxation, the burden of which increases when prices decline.

The adjustment of money rates of wages to the fall in the cost of living is usually effected only after a time lag; consequently real wages are higher and constitute a greater charge on industry than before. The process of wage reduction is accompanied by strained industrial relations and increase in the number of disputes. Markets are depressed since, especially for durable goods, potential purchasers withhold their demand in anticipation of satisfying their requirements at still lower prices.

Wage and also salary earners who have the good fortune to remain fully employed during depression of industry caused by monetary shortage and declining prices usually enjoy increase in real wages and salaries. Each fall in the cost of living increases their standard of living, and although they will often be compelled to accept reductions in money wages these lag behind the price movement; the fully employed worker, therefore, tends to retain some benefit from the declining cost of living. As has been indicated, however, the reductions of money wages with which he is faced often result in strained industrial relations and may involve the losses of a strike or lock-out. Also the depression of industry involves many workers in short time or unemployment, and in effecting the full balance sheet the losses of these workers must be set against the gain in real wages by those who are fully employed.[1]

The investor in Government and other public loans and in industrial debenture and other fixed interest securities receives increasing real value in interest as prices fall. Also he enjoys increases in the market value of his securities and in the real value of any loans which are repaid. Investors, however, who distribute their capital between fixed interest securities and ordinary shares are liable to find their gain from the former balanced by the decline in the rates of dividend and the market value of the latter, which reflect the conditions of industrial depression. Also some of the gains from holding fixed interest securities are withdrawn by higher real rates of taxation to meet public debt charges.

[1] The close causal relation between the money factor and unemployment, with special reference to the situation in various countries during the years 1925, 1926, and 1927, is shown by M. Henri Füss in an article on "Money and Unemployment", *International Labour Review*, November 1927.

Falling prices from monetary causes have been a feature of the world situation since 1926. Great Britain has experienced not only a depression of prices due to the internal level being about 10 per cent. above world gold prices when the gold standard was restored in 1925, but also the decline from world causes. The decline has undoubtedly aggravated the industrial depression and has been a cause of industrial disputes and wage reductions. It is true that British trade has been injured by other factors, especially the development of industries under the protection of tariffs in countries which formerly imported manufactured goods from Great Britain. Clearly this cannot be remedied by a policy of monetary stability. But the situation has been rendered still more serious by the effects of the monetary factor on the price-level. The disastrous position in the cotton and woollen textile industries, culminating in the disputes and wage reductions of 1929 and 1930, was intensified by this factor. Nor is it in the power of British industry to deal with this difficulty. Even the British banks and the Government can make only a partial contribution to its solution. This is one of the real difficulties of all political parties when considering remedies for unemployment, that it is due in part to world monetary factors which cannot be removed by national measures, but only by international cooperation.

A rising price-level due to monetary causes has a converse effect on the business world, the wage earner, and the investor. The burden of fixed charges on industry is reduced, stocks of finished goods appreciate in money value, while owing to time lag in adjusting wage rates to the rise in prices real wages fall, i.e. the real cost of labour declines. Consequently industry is stimulated, production tends to be over-developed, markets are brisk, and there is little unemployment. Fully employed wage earners experience a decline in real wages which is offset, at least partially, by reduction in short time and in total unemployment. Employers are especially anxious to avoid disputes when industry is prosperous; they are, however, usually unwilling to accede to the full demands of the workers; they fear this would increase the difficulties of industry if, after a time, prosperity declines and wage reductions become necessary. Consequently industrial relations are strained and strikes and lock-outs tend to increase in number and severity. Rising prices also reduce the real value of fixed interest rates and thus favour the borrower at the expense of the lender.

Preference for rising prices, stability of prices or falling prices will depend on the economic position of the individual; some consider that a gradually rising price-level is most advantageous to the community as it progressively reduces the real burden of old debts and gives a stimulus to industry. Others regard a slowly declining price-level as being preferable, for real wages increase without the necessity for struggling to secure increases in money wages. This preference is strengthened if adequate benefits are secured to the unemployed, but this again is offset by the demoralisation of prolonged unemployment.

The balance of advantages seems to be on the side of stability of prices if a policy of control is adopted.

Both rising and falling prices involve fortuitous gains or losses to different classes of the community. This increases friction, especially in industrial relations, but also between social classes. By a policy which ensures reasonable price stability, the menace of over-development and undue depression of industry is largely removed.

Many of the consequences of instability outlined above may set up unfortunate international repercussions. But there are also direct international consequences which strengthen the case for stability. Loans, debts, and interest rates between nations, as between individuals, change their real value when the price-level falls or rises. Therefore the real burden of international obligations is arbitrarily altered and relative indebtedness becomes quite different from that intended by the contracting parties. Consequently international friction and misunderstanding may develop. A striking example is the British war debt to the United States. This was funded in 1923 at £945,205,000, but as a result of the subsequent fall of 30 per cent. in prices, the real weight of the debt in 1930 had increased by over £250,000,000 despite the fact that £35,000,000 had been paid to the United States. Many repayments to the United States are now being made in gold, which has twice the value of the money borrowed. True, Britain has been compensated for some of her loss to the United States by gains from her continental debtors. But such arbitrary distortion of international monetary obligations can hardly be justified. Thus the careful adjustment of Germany's reparation payments in the Young settlement has been seriously vitiated

M

by the subsequent fall in prices, and the real burden of Germany's obligations has been raised considerably above that agreed upon after weeks of intricate discussion at the Hague Conference. This may involve a further revision of reparation payments with inevitable strain on international relations.

There is evidently an unanswerable case for monetary stability as a means of reducing social and industrial unrest within each country and of removing a menace to international peace.

INTERNATIONAL FACTORS CAUSING INSTABILITY

The gold standard—or its equivalents, the gold bullion standard and the gold exchange standard—closely links together the monetary systems of a large number of countries.[1] A factor causing instability in one country is likely to result in similar reactions elsewhere. Thus a monetary change resulting in a rise in the level of prices in one country tends to induce a rise in other countries. The rise in prices makes it more difficult for the country to export goods while, on the other hand, its imports increase. This results in an unfavourable balance of trade, which disturbs the rates of foreign exchange, and this, if continued, is met by an export of gold. This export of gold tends to bring down the level of prices within the country and raise it abroad. This tends to bring prices in the different countries into equivalence again, although at a higher level than before the initial change.

[1] A detailed account of the difference between the gold standard as operated before the war and the new British post-war gold standard is given by Mr. William Adams Brown, Jr., in *England and the New Gold Standard*, London, 1929.

It is, of course, quite possible for a country to break away from the monetary systems of other countries and to keep its own internal price-level largely independent of external factors. Thus British prices were relatively stable in 1922, 1923, and 1924, when many European countries were experiencing wild fluctuations. But though the British price-level was relatively stable, the foreign exchange rates reflected the fluctuations abroad, and foreign trade was hampered by these fluctuations. With the widespread restoration of the gold standard, the foreign exchange rates of different countries are kept stable, but the internal price-level of each country is liable to be affected by monetary conditions abroad. In other words, the value of gold is determined by the cumulative conditions of demand for and supply of gold in the different countries, and therefore the value of the monetary unit and the commodity price-level of each country reflects changes in these conditions.

The chief international factors causing instability of monetary values and therefore affecting the price-levels in different countries by the processes indicated above are[1]:

1. Variations in the level of prices in any country as a result of changes in the volume of bank credits.
2. Changes in the demand for gold for monetary purposes by any country or group of countries.
3. Changes in the supply of gold for monetary purposes, especially the production of new gold.

[1] Cf. *Industrial Fluctuations*, chap. viii, by Professor A. C. Pigou, London, 1929.

The first of these factors is often closely associated with the various phases of the business cycle. An increase or decrease in the volume of bank credit resulting in a rise or fall in prices in one country tends to cause a similar development in other countries by generating the sequence of reactions already described. Therefore industrial activity in some countries may be stimulated or depressed by the action taken in others with regard to bank credit. Evidently it is desirable that injurious consequences should be prevented by international cooperation. Otherwise a country may find itself hampered by the course of monetary events abroad: a fall in prices may be forced upon it at a time when it was endeavouring to maintain stability or give its industry the encouragement of a rise in prices.

True, the control of bank credit and through this the smoothing out of the booms and depressions of the business cycle is largely a national problem. But whereas at present, with occasional exceptions, each country acts independently, cooperation could be the means of securing the maximum of benefit with a minimum of injury.

The development of cooperation, demanding considerable caution for the effective control of bank credit, has not yet become a recognised technique. High hopes were raised by the success with which the Federal Reserve Authorities in the United States applied a policy of credit control to keep the price-level and business activity reasonably stable and prosperous during the years 1921 to the autumn of 1929.[1]

---

[1] Price stabilisation was not an avowed policy of the Federal Reserve Authorities. However, in giving evidence in 1927 before the Com-

It was even considered that the problem of industrial fluctuations had been largely solved and that henceforth the business cycle would be a phenomenon of only historical interest. The course of wholesale prices in the United States during this period is shown by the following official annual averages (base 1926 = 100)[1] :

Year	Index	Year	Index
1921	97·6	1926	100
1922	96·7	1927	95·4
1923	100·6	1928	97·7
1924	98·1	1929 June	96·4
1925	103·5	1929 September	97·5

Thus, for almost nine years, the variation of the index was rarely more than 3 or 4 per cent. from the base. This stability is all the more remarkable in view of the wide fluctuations in prices and the changes in monetary policy in many other countries during the same period. It seemed, therefore, that the Federal Reserve Authorities had solved the problem of price stability and the trade cycle, and that other countries had only to apply similar methods in order to prevent the development of booms and depressions.

That the problem is yet not solved is indicated by subsequent events. The crash on the New York Stock Exchange in the autumn of 1929 was followed by a steady fall in prices and depression of industry in

mittee on Banking and Currency of the United States House of Representatives (Sixty-ninth Congress, First Session on H.R. 7895), Governor Strong stated that since the reaction of 1921 the administration of the Federal Reserve System had been directed towards the maintenance of price stability (vol. i, p. 307).

[1] Bureau of Labour Statistics indexes.

the United States, but which spread rapidly to Great Britain, Germany, Japan, and other countries. The following figures show the decline in the United States wholesale price index during recent months (base 1926 = 100):

Date	Index	Date	Index
1929 July	98·0	1930 March	90·8
September	97·5	June	86·8
December	94·2	September	84·2

This fall in prices and the industrial depression took place in spite of efforts of the banking authorities and the Hoover Administration to maintain prosperity. Evidently the trade cycle cannot be controlled by manipulation of bank credit alone, since it is a consequence of other factors in addition to monetary conditions. Nevertheless the United States has made a considerable contribution by its experiments in control of credit during the last decade, and further progress on these lines, with international cooperation, should lead gradually to the suppression of extremes of industrial boom and depression.

Changes in the demand for gold for monetary purposes by any country or group of countries may cause considerable international dislocation. Independent national action undertaken without consideration of international repercussions may involve injury abroad. This may be the result of the application of different policies and represent a form of economic conflict which should be restrained by international cooperation.

Examples of such changes in demand would be the adoption of the gold standard by any country or an increase or decrease in the ratio of the gold reserve to note issue. Thus the establishment of the gold standard by Germany after the Franco-German War of 1870 led to large imports of gold into that country especially during the years 1871–73. This, and increased demand for gold by other countries, contributed to a rise in the value of gold and a fall in prices.

In recent years difficulties have resulted from the policy of particular countries in retaining or establishing unnecessarily large gold reserves. In fact, there has been a scramble for gold by certain countries, and the larger perspective of the general welfare has been displaced by narrow considerations of national self-interest. Reasonable increases have been made in the gold reserves of some countries in the process of restoring stability to their monetary systems. In other countries, excessive quantities of gold have been accumulated. This is true particularly of France whose gold reserves were greatly increased in 1928, 1929, and 1930. Also a more constructive gold policy by the Federal Reserve Authorities of the United States would have done much to ease the situation. These two countries, in fact, hold considerably more than half the world's monetary gold; Great Britain holds only about 7 per cent., and Germany about 5 per cent. The United States holds a stock over six times, and France nearly three times, that of Great Britain, despite the latter's important rôle in the world's monetary system. The table below gives statistics of the monetary gold stocks held by

France, Germany, Great Britain, Italy, and the United
States from 1925 to 1929:

MONETARY GOLD STOCKS OF VARIOUS COUNTRIES,
1925–1929 [1]

(*In Millions of Dollars*)

Date	France	Germany	Great Britain	Italy	United States
1925	1,066	303	712	221	4,399
1926	1,066	452	743	223	4,492
1927	1,065	460	750	239	4,379
1928	1,259	666	754	266	4,141
1929	1,631	560	719	273	4,284

It might be thought that the transfer of gold from
one country to another would have little effect on
the *world* level of prices, but merely cause temporary,
and perhaps inconvenient, changes in the levels of
prices in various countries. The Gold Delegation of the
Financial Committee of the League indicate that "if
the distribution of gold is the result of excessive or
abnormal competition by a few countries, or if it has
the effect of sterilising important amounts of monetary
stocks, serious consequences will arise affecting the
general level of prices".[2] If the gold imported by France
and other countries had been used as basis for increasing currency and credit, prices would have risen in
these countries and have fallen in the countries which
had lost gold. Actually much of the imported gold has
simply been hoarded and has not been used as basis
for currency or credit. Its value to the world's monetary
system has been little greater that if the gold had been

[1] *Interim Report of the Gold Delegation*, pp. 114-15, data compiled
by A. Loveday. Figures for end of year.   [2] *Interim Report*, p. 17.

left in the mines; the same is true of part of the stock held by the United States. The supply of gold used effectively for monetary purposes has been reduced and the level of prices has consequently fallen.

The trend of world prices since 1925 is shown by the index numbers of wholesale prices given in the table on page 186. The fall has been most marked and continuous in Great Britain, Sweden and Switzerland, and also in Italy and Japan, where currency and credit changes also affected the level of prices. It will be noted that the large accessions of gold to France from 1928 to 1930 did not result in a rise in commodity prices. The acceleration of the fall in all countries between 1929 and 1930 will also be noted.

The downward trend of prices has been the result of non-monetary and also of monetary causes, including undue absorption of gold by certain countries and world shortage of gold production to meet the growing requirements of industry and trade. Prices would have fallen somewhat from this second cause alone, but the fall has been aggravated by lack of economy and mal-distribution of the supply available.

It is likely that the exceptional scramble for gold by certain countries has now almost run its course, and that little further influence on the level of prices may be expected from this cause. "The most effective distribution of gold is likely to become of steadily increasing importance in future years as the supplies of new gold become smaller. It may, however, be expected that the special causes which have determined the gold movements of the last few years will gradually work themselves out, and that the possibility of an

INDEX NUMBERS OF WHOLESALE PRICES IN VARIOUS COUNTRIES, 1925–1930[1]

(Base, 1913 = 100)

Date	France	Germany	Great Britain[2]	Italy[3]	Japan	Netherlands	Sweden	Switzer-land	United States
1925	550	142	159	596	267	173	161	162	148
1926	703	134	148	603	237	162	149	145	143
1927	617	138	142	495	225	165	146	142	137
1928	620	140	140	462	226	167	148	145	140
1929	610	137	137	446	220	159	140	141	138
1930	532	125	120	383	185[4]	131	122	126	124

[1] Compiled from figures published in the League of Nations *Monthly Bulletin of Statistics.*
The indexes are yearly averages.
[2] Board of Trade series.
[3] "Bachi" series.
[4] January to October.

optimum distribution being achieved later by means of intelligent cooperation will steadily increase."[1] The world shortage of gold production to meet the growing requirements of industry and trade will prob ably have a depressing effect on prices for many years. And this effect will be accentuated unless a more enlightened policy is adopted by countries which hold large percentages of the world's monetary gold.

Already the wholesale prices of many important commodities have fallen to the pre-war level. In December 1930 the British general level of wholesale prices was only 10 per cent. above the pre-war level, having fallen over 15 per cent. in the preceding eighteen months. Considering the declines in the price-level in preceding years, it is small wonder that industry is depressed and the volume of unemployment has swelled to almost unprecedented proportions. Unless a reasonable policy of international cooperation can be evolved there seems every prospect that prices will continue to decline, that in a few years price-levels below that of 1914 will be reached, and that the process of decline will be attended by continued industrial depression with only short minor recoveries.

INTERNATIONAL COOPERATION TO SECURE STABILITY

The adoption of the gold standard by a number of countries ensures, within narrow limits, the stability of the exchange rates between their currencies.[2] Minor

[1] *Interim Report of the Gold Delegation*, p. 18.
[2] Stability of exchange rates facilitates international trade but is of less importance in the economic life of a country than stability of its internal price-level. The relative importance to any country

departures from the parity of exchange occur, but as soon as they become considerable they are corrected by movements of gold. But although the exchange rates remain stable the price-level of each country is influenced by changes in prices abroad. With the gold standard it is impossible for a country to maintain stability of its internal price-level if the purchasing power of gold is changing abroad. A country could, of course, abandon the gold standard and adopt a policy of maintaining stable prices at home, but if prices were changing abroad the rates of foreign exchange would then be unstable. With the gold standard an attempt to maintain prices at home when prices are falling abroad would result in an excess of imports over exports, foreign exchange rates would become unfavourable, and gold exports would follow. This and the consequent reduction of credit would cause prices at home to fall until international equilibrium had been restored. Each country acting alone is powerless to shield itself against movements in particular countries or against general trends abroad.

The need for international cooperation is widely recognised both in Great Britain and abroad. Thus international action to prevent undue fluctuations in the purchasing power of gold was recommended as long ago as 1922 by the Genoa Conference. In 1929 the International Federation of Trade Unions, representing nearly fourteen million workers, recommended in its economic policy that "every effort should be made to keep as stable as possible the purchasing power of

of internal price stability and stability of the foreign exchanges varies according to the relation between the size of its home and its foreign markets.

gold in terms of goods and services and thus help to secure stability of prices, productive activity, and fuller employment of the workers".

The British Labour Party at its Birmingham Congress, October 1928, passed a resolution on currency which included the following passage: "International action is required to secure at one and the same time stability of the exchanges and stability of the purchasing power of money." They therefore recommended that Britain should give a lead in this direction. A similar view was expressed by the British Committee on Industry and Trade in the following recommendation: "The fact that such a prospect (i.e. shortage of monetary gold and falling prices) is at least possible, and that a continued decline in prices usually has a depressing influence on industrial activity, adds weight to our recommendation that all practicable and suitable steps should be taken by concerted action among the central Banks towards economising the use and stabilising the value of gold."[1]

In the present section a review will be given of the possibilities of securing monetary stability by international cooperation. Before, however, considering the measures which may be taken it is necessary to decide what criterion of stability to adopt. There is considerable support for the adoption of an index of wholesale prices.[2]

[1] *Final Report of the Committee on Industry and Trade*, London, 1929, p. 57.
[2] It would be more logical to take a retail price index, but this does not directly include various important commodities used in construction, e.g. iron and steel, building materials, and the indirect effect of changes in their prices on the retail index is felt only after a lengthy time lag. Many of the problems involved in the choice

In calculating such an index the cost is taken of given quantities of representative commodities, the quantities depending on the relative importance of each commodity; thus the index might include a ton of coal, a ton of pig-iron, specified quantities of wheat, oil, rubber, timber, paper, cloth, and so on. To stabilise the monetary unit in terms of such an index would mean that at different dates the pound sterling, for example, would have the same purchasing power over the group of commodities included in the index. The price of each commodity might change, some becoming dearer and others cheaper; but increases in the price of some commodities would be compensated by decreases in others, so that the purchasing power of the pound would remain unchanged.

Some may think it would be preferable to aim at securing stability of production rather than stability of prices, but money is used as a medium of exchange and a standard of value and is not directly related to production. However, the maintenance of stability of purchasing power of the monetary unit would make a considerable contribution to stability of production

of a criterion of stability are discussed by Mr. R. G. Hawtrey in "Money and Index Numbers" (*Journal of the Royal Statistical Society*, Part I, 1930); in this paper the idea is advanced of stabilising the monetary unit in terms of human effort. Cf. also Mr. Hawtrey's *Monetary Reconstruction*, London, 1926, p. 165.)

The construction of index numbers involves many technical and practical problems, among which are the selection of the commodities and services to be included, the fixing of the appropriate quantity of each commodity, the collection of the prices, and methods of computation; also changes in the commodities and quantities may be necessary from time to time as their importance in use is modified. Statistical technique is, however, developed sufficiently to cope with these problems.

by avoiding the undue expansion or contraction of production which rising or falling prices induce.

It will be recognised that absolute stability of the price-level could not be attained in practice. The aim of monetary policy should, however, be to restrict short-period fluctuations within narrow limits and to prevent-long period downward or upward trends.

International cooperation with the object of maintaining price stability would involve selection of some index or indices as a guide to monetary policy. These might be either the national wholesale price indices of the various countries or a world index might be computed. Probably the former would be adequate as a general guide, especially during the first years of cooperation.

In considering measures of cooperation to secure reasonable stability of purchasing power of the monetary unit, distinction must be drawn between:

1. Trade-cycle fluctuations.
2. Mal-utilisation of the available supplies of monetary gold.
3. Long-period shortage or surplus of gold.

Each of these involves special problems and demands special remedies.

1. *Trade-Cycle Fluctuations.*

Trade-cycle fluctuations with wide variations in prices may occur either with long-period stability of prices, or with a long-period trend of falling or of rising prices. But trade-cycle depressions are likely to be especially severe and prolonged if the general long-period trend of prices is downwards as at the present time. Control of trade-cycle fluctuations is partly an internal national problem. There are, however, international repercussions, and control within each country would be much facilitated by international coordination of policy.

The causes of trade cycles are numerous and have been discussed in a vast literature on the subject. One of the potent influences is the volume of credit and the effect it exerts on the level of prices. The volume of credit is largely determined by the monetary policy of the banks, especially of the central bank, and in gold-standard countries the gold reserve has been a determining factor in ease or stringency of credit. An opportune easing of credit may prevent the development of industrial depression and fall of prices, while an appropriate restriction of credit tends to restrain the business world from over-expansion and to prevent a sharp rise in the price-level. In determining the right moment for the easing or restricting of credit the central bank must endeavour to *anticipate* the potential trend of business activity and prices. A movement of gold from the reserve does not give early enough warning of an approaching crisis.[1] Nor would monetary stability be likely to be effected by a policy of waiting until a price movement had begun before taking measures to counteract it. To adopt an automatic system based on a specified movement of prices or of reserve

[1] "The too ready acceptance of reserve proportions as the guide to credit policy was the real cause of the trade cycle before the war. Reserve proportions gave too tardy a warning of a credit expansion. . . ." (*Currency and Credit*, by R. G. Hawtrey, London, 1923).

ratios would result in failure as these movements are often too late.[1]

Effective anticipation demands judgment about the various economic factors operating, both monetary and non-monetary; this is facilitated by systematic examination of a wide range of economic statistics, especially those which enable forecasts to be made of probable trends. Special attention would be given, not only to the price-level, but also to indexes of production, employment, stocks of commodities, and trends of trade in relation to the credit situation.[2]

It will be recognised that credit control can hardly be expected to prevent some fluctuations of prices or to eliminate trade-cycle fluctuations.[3] The complexity of the economic structure is such that errors of judgment by those responsible for the control of credit are unavoidable. Also non-monetary factors such as variations in harvests are disturbing elements. Nevertheless, the present greater understanding of the factors operating, the compilation of more adequate data on the business situation, and, above all, the development

---

[1] Cf. J. M. Keynes, *A Tract on Monetary Reform*, London, 1923, p. 187, and R. G. Hawtrey, *Monetary Reconstruction*, London, 1926, p. 105.

[2] Considerable progress has been made during recent years in the compilation and analysis of the relevant series of business statistics as a basis for forecasting trade-cycle trends. An indication of the range of statistics which must be brought under review is given in *Business Cycles and Business Measurements*, by Carl Snyder, New York, 1927.

[3] Special difficulties arise in the endeavour to direct the flow of credit so as to maintain equilibrium between the different industries themselves, and between industry as a whole and other branches of economic activity. Also the power of a central bank to influence the volume of credit varies according to circumstances; it is greater during a period of strain than during the preceding periods.

of experience, will facilitate measures of credit control by a central bank at the right time and in the right degree. These measures, by maintaining reasonable stability of prices, will tend greatly to diminish the severity of trade-cycle fluctuations. The attitude of business men would be modified if they were convinced that a policy of price stability was being pursued. They would be no longer subject to waves of exaggerated optimism or undue depression based on anticipation of a rise or fall in the price-level. This would assist the maintenance of stability both of prices and of industrial activity.

The chief methods by which a central bank can affect the volume of credit are by raising or lowering the discount rate and by selling or buying securities.[1] Changes in the discount rate not only affect trade borrowings at home, but the willingness of foreigners to retain or withdraw liquid assets from the country, and this in turn affects the gold reserve. Also the situation is affected by changes in discount rates abroad. Here the establishment of international cooperation would be of value. So long as each country pursues an independent discount policy, one country, which needs to ease its credit situation at home by a lowering of the discount rate to avoid trade depression, may find it impossible to take the necessary action owing to the relatively high rates prevailing abroad.

There would be much advantage in cooperation between a group of countries which would act together

[1] Hitherto these measures have often been applied too late to prevent considerable fluctuation in prices and in business activity. Cf. an article on "Tardy Discount Policy", by Professor Gustav Cassel, in *Skandinaviska Kreditaktiebolaget*, July 1930.

in the general interest. At present each country frequently pursues a policy which, often unwittingly,
conflicts with the necessities of the situation abroad,
and consequently inflicts economic injury. Tentative
steps in cooperation have been taken in recent years by
the central banks of several countries, but progress
needs to be much accelerated if consistent results are
to be obtained.[1]

2. Mal-utilisation of the Available Supplies of Monetary Gold.

The decline in the price-level during recent years
and industrial depression which many countries have
experienced are not due mainly to immediate world
shortage of monetary gold. The supplies available are
adequate under present conditions of monetary policy
to maintain a stable purchasing power of gold provided they were reasonably distributed. Unfortunately
distribution is far from rational. Certain countries,
notably the United States, and, during the last two or
three years, France, have withdrawn from monetary
use, or, to use Sir Henry Strakosch's expression, have
"sterilised" large quantities of gold.

As already shown, the United States has a hoard

---

[1] An account of the measures of cooperation is given by Paul
Einzig in *The Bank for International Settlements*, London, 1930,
Chapter II, "Cooperation between Central Banks". That cooperation is yet far from adequate is indicated in an article in the *Statist*,
September 28, 1929. The following observation was made on the
raising of the British Bank Rate in September 1929 in consequence
of the high money rates prevailing in New York during the frenzy
of the speculative boom: "The circumstances which forced the
Bank of England to impose what is virtually a panic rate when
every index in the domestic situation calls for easier credit conditions is a damning commentary on that intelligent cooperation
between central banks which is supposed to be taking place. . . ."

of gold in the vaults of the Federal Reserve Banks which is worth over £800,000,000, or more than one-third of the world's store of monetary gold. About £300,000,000 is in excess of the minimum legal requirements. Allowing a reasonable margin above minimum legal requirements, a considerable sum, nearly £150,000,000, is unnecessary surplus which could be released without involving the United States in the slightest monetary shortage or economic difficulty, and could be used to maintain stability of the world price-level.

France, which had accumulated large foreign short-term credits during the depreciation of the franc, began in 1928 to use these assets for the purchase of gold. This was imported to augment the gold reserve of the Bank of France, which by the end of 1930 had grown to the enormous total of about £430,000,000. This represented a cover of 70 per cent. of the French bank-note issue, and about 60 per cent. of all sight engagements, whereas a minimum of only 35 per cent. is required by law.[1] The Bank of England's gold reserve at the same time was about £150,000,000, representing a cover of 41 per cent. of the note issue. Evidently, if the British reserve was at all adequate to meet her much larger cheque circulation and her international financial obligations, the French reserve was far in excess of requirements. The excess is probably over £200,000,000.

Unfortunately, neither France nor the United States has yet shown clear signs of adopting a more liberal policy. Were they to cooperate with the other

[1] If foreign sight assets held by the Bank are added to the gold reserve, the cover of the note issue was over 100 per cent.

gold-using countries in effecting a better distribution
and utilisation of the world's monetary gold, there would
be hope of a cessation of price-decline and a rapid
return to business prosperity. It seems unlikely that
the United States will endeavour to secure further
important increases in its gold reserves. On the other
hand, France in the summer of 1930 had short-
term credits abroad to a total which was still over
£200,000,000. If, as in the previous three years, these
credits are converted into gold and large sums imported into France, the strain on the international,
commercial, and financial system will be serious, and
recovery from the industrial depression in many
countries further delayed. The pursuance of this policy
would also mean that France would burden herself
with a still greater uneconomic load of gold, far in
excess of any reasonable requirements as basis for
increasing her currency and credit or for strengthening
her position as an international financial centre.

Deliberately, to continue on these lines with knowledge of the international repercussions would be no
less than an act of economic warfare. On the other
hand, uncertainty about the consequences or how to
prevent them could be remedied by international
enquiry, education, and cooperation. It is hoped that
by these means France will speedily recognise her
responsibilities in the financial family of nations, and,
instead of continuing this injurious drain of gold, will
convert her foreign liquid assets into long-term loans.[1]
This, together with the adoption of a broad international

---

[1] The French Minister of Finance, in a speech at Epinal on August 2,
1930, indicated that some encouragement was being given to French
investors to adopt this policy. *The Times*, August 4, 1930, p. 9.

policy of monetary cooperation by the United States, would brighten the financial and industrial outlook for the years immediately ahead. By cooperation a reasonable distribution of monetary gold between the different countries could gradually be effected. This might involve an increase in the gold reserves of some countries and a decrease in those of others. The requirements of each country would demand separate consideration. To base the gold reserve of each country on its population or production would be unsatisfactory. Since, as will be indicated later, the main purpose of gold under present conditions is to effect international balance of payments, countries with a relatively large foreign trade and financial relations would require a relatively greater reserve than countries with smaller international obligations. Experience in cooperation would gradually enable the most economical distribution of the stock of monetary gold to be effected.

3. *Long-period Shortage or Surplus of Gold.*

The effect on the price-level of long-period shortage or surplus of gold is usually slower, but much more prolonged than that of trade-cycle fluctuations. Such shortage or surplus depends on the relation between the rate of increase of production and trade, growth of the stock of monetary gold especially by new output of the mines, and changes in monetary policy. Assuming there to be no change in monetary policy, an increase of production and trade at a greater rate than the stock of monetary gold would result in shortage of currency and credit and consequently in a declining price-level. The converse is equally true, and since it is highly improbable that growth of the stock of monetary gold will permanently keep pace exactly with economic progress, deliberate measures must be taken if the world is to enjoy the advantages of stable purchasing power of its monetary unit. As all indications point to a world shortage of monetary gold, attention is directed here mainly to measures for dealing with this situation. The remedies for a surplus would generally be the reverse of these measures.

The prospect of a world shortage of monetary gold is often based on the assumption that production and trade are expanding at the rate of about 3 per cent. per annum, i.e. at the same rate as that estimated for the latter half of the nineteenth century and the early years of the twentieth century. Probably this rate of expansion will not be maintained, but even if it fell as low as 2 per cent. there would be still the menace of gold shortage. The present stock of monetary gold has been estimated at nearly £2,300,000,000. Annual production is about £80,000,000, of which rather less than half is absorbed for non-monetary purposes by India and for industrial use. Thus the stock of monetary gold is now increasing at a rate of less than 2 per cent. per annum. In the course of the next decade the rate of growth will fall considerably except in the unlikely event of important gold discoveries or great technical improvements in extraction. It is estimated that the output of the South African mines, which now constitutes more than half of the total world production, will decline rapidly after about 1932, owing to exhaustion of various mines. As has been seen, the shortage is aggravated by mal-distribution of the stock available, and there is always the possibility of large new demands by Oriental countries, especially China, if they should adopt the gold standard.[1]

It might be supposed that a shortage of gold and a fall in the price-level would make gold-mining more profitable, and therefore lead to a compensating increase of gold production. True, after a fall in prices each ounce of gold produced will purchase more in goods and services, and this would tend to make gold production more profitable. But the effect on production will probably be far from sufficient to prevent a decline in prices, especially in view of the increased costs of extraction as the mines approach exhaustion.

Measures of international cooperation to meet this shortage might be either to operate on the side of supply by adjusting the output of gold to the growing needs of industry and trade, or to meet these needs on the side of demand for gold by a modification of monetary policy. Both these measures are here discussed, although the latter method is preferred as being more practicable and adaptable to changing monetary conditions.

A plan for maintaining monetary stability by regulating the output of gold to the needs of industry and commerce was formulated by the late Professor Lehrfeldt.[2] He proposed that the output of gold should

---

[1] On the other hand the shortage will be rendered less acute if, in consequence of a fall in the rate of population growth and reductions in hours of labour as productivity increases, the rate of expansion of production and trade declines.

[2] The plan is described in some detail in a memorandum by R. A. Lehrfeldt, Professor of Economics at the University of the Witwatersrand, Johannesburg: "Controlling the Output of Gold" (League of Nations Economic and Financial Commission, Document E.F./146, October 11, 1926).

be controlled, with a view to stabilising its value, by a powerful financial Commission. The Commission, which would require a capital of one or two hundred millions sterling, would consist of representatives of the chief gold-producing countries, and also of non-producers. It would use its capital to acquire control over all gold-mining undertakings, that is, it would be an international trust with a complete monopoly of production. It would require powers for the compulsory purchase of existing mines, and of newly discovered areas at reasonable valuations. Its policy would be to increase or reduce the output of gold according to the needs of industry and trade. This would, however, become progressively more difficult with the exhaustion of mines, and the scheme would involve a growing burden of production at a loss. The plan would be of more value if the world were faced with a surplus instead of a shortage of monetary gold.

Regulation of the demand for gold by a modification of monetary policy seems a more practicable remedy.[1] There are many ways of diminishing the demand for monetary gold. One is the abandonment of the use of gold coin. This course, adopted during the War by many of the leading industrial countries for quite other reasons, has considerably relieved the post-war shortage of gold. The general satisfaction which the paper currency gives in these countries is likely to have a wide influence. Thus it may tend to induce

[1] A tax on gold for industrial uses has been suggested as a means of increasing the supply of monetary gold, e.g. by Professor E. W. Kemmerer, see *The American Economic Review*, vol. xviii, No. 1, Supplement, March 1928, Papers and Proceedings of the Fortieth Annual Meeting of the American Economic Association, Washington, D.C., December 1927.

countries which still use gold coinage to adopt a paper currency. It may also influence certain countries, where the habit of hoarding currency is common and where a section of the community might prefer gold to paper for this purpose, to refrain from reintroducing circulation of gold coins.

A second measure of economy in the use of gold would be an extension of the practice of concentrating the gold reserve of the banking system in the central bank of each country. The result of this and of the abandonment of gold coinage would mean that the sole real use of monetary gold would be to settle international balances of payment. The League's Gold Delegation express the hope that "the concentration of monetary gold in the reserves of central banks, and its limitation as a means of payment to international transactions, may shortly become generalised. . . ."[1]

The gold-exchange standard, which has been applied extensively since the war, is another method of economising the world's stock of monetary gold. A country which adopts this system, instead of building up a gold reserve, establishes reserves in liquid assets abroad in the currencies of countries on a gold standard. This is an economical and effective method, but is open to the objection that foreign assets would be liable to seizure on an outbreak of war. Consequently there has been a tendency for the gold-exchange standard to be replaced by the gold-bullion standard. However, with the growth of international confidence, an economy of gold could be effected, even by countries with gold reserves, if they would reduce the amount of this reserve and

[1] *Interim Report,* p. 18.

compensate the reduction by an increase in foreign assets.

All these methods of economising gold are of value, but they would be inadequate to meet a serious pro- longed gold shortage. For this a more fundamental remedy is necessary. The most effective one would be to change the relation between the gold reserve and the volume of currency.[1] In many countries the central bank is required to keep a legal reserve of a specified proportion of its note issue, but in some countries this may be held partly in gold and partly in foreign assets. This reserve is often between 30 and 40 per cent. in different countries, and the central banks naturally find it necessary, also, to maintain a margin above the minimum legal reserve. Actually the gold reserves held by the different central banks represent a cover of a little over 40 per cent. of the note issue and other sight liabilities, the minimum legal gold cover being in practice about 32 per cent.[2]

The practice common to many countries of requiring a legal minimum of about 32 per cent. in gold has no logical basis. It has largely developed in imitation of the British minimum adopted a century ago, when the financial system was less highly organised than at present and when gold coins were in circulation. Other countries adopted a minimum percentage similar to the British without enquiring whether they needed as large a cover as Britain whose foreign trade and

[1] In addition to this measure and the other means mentioned of economising gold, shortage would be relieved by increases in the rapidity of circulation, for example, by more extensive use of cheques in various countries.

[2] *Interim Report of the Gold Delegation*, p. 14.

finance were of such predominant importance. Also, with the abandonment of gold coinage central banks are likely to be faced with a smaller demand for the conversion of notes into gold, and consequently the gold reserve ratio might reasonably be smaller than that necessary before the war. "The main function of the legal minimum is thus to establish confidence, active operations being conducted, not with this minimum, but with the additional margin which is held in gold or assets immediately convertible into gold. The minimum is largely conventional, and a considerable economy could quite certainly be accomplished were the current accepted minima reduced. We believe that this could be done without in any way weakening the general credit structure."[1]

If the central bank of one country alone were to reduce its reserve ratio of gold to notes, for example, by increasing its note issue without increasing its gold reserve, the stability of its credit might be suspected abroad. But this would be avoided if the central banks of the chief countries acted simultaneously in this way.[2] By this means the menace of the long-period shortage of monetary gold could be removed. When the shortage began to cause a decline in prices the central banks would undertake to reduce the minimum reserve ratio by an agreed proportion and to refrain from compensating this reduction by increasing the relation between the minimum reserve and the actual reserve. Suppose in Great Britain that before an agree-

[1] *Interim Report of the Gold Delegation*, p. 19.
[2] To enable central banks to operate this system the legislation on minimum reserve ratios in the various countries would require modification.

ment to make a reduction in the reserve ratio the note issue was £360,000,000, minimum reserve £120,000,000, i.e. 33⅓ per cent. of the note issue, and the actual reserve £150,000,000, i.e. 25 per cent. more than the minimum reserve; suppose also that an agreement was reached to reduce the minimum reserve ratio to 30 per cent. This would mean that the note issue could be raised to £400,000,000 with the existing gold reserves. Similar changes would be made in other countries. Therefore, on the assumption that the central banks had correctly calculated the percentage by which the reserve ratios should be reduced, this increase in the note issue would prevent the fall in prices and supply the currency needed to meet the requirements of expanding production and trade. A surplus of gold and rising prices could be neutralised by reversing the process.[1]

[1] Measures of price stabilisation have been proposed for single countries, by Professor Irving Fisher for the United States, in *The Money Illusion*, New York, 1928 (see pp. 190–1) and in *Stabilising the Dollar*, New York, 1920, and by J. M. Keynes for Great Britain, in *A Tract on Monetary Reform*, London, 1923, i.e. before the situation was modified by the return of Great Britain and many other countries to the gold standard. These measures would aim at securing price stability at the expense of stability of the foreign exchanges. Professor Fisher's proposal is for a "compensated dollar," i.e. a dollar which would not be convertible into a permanently fixed weight of gold as at present, but into such weight as would be officially declared from time to time. During a period of gold shortage and falling prices the weight of gold which a dollar represented would be reduced; consequently more dollar notes could be issued on a given gold reserve and the fall in price would be counteracted by this increase in currency. Mr. Keynes advocated that the Bank of England instead of buying or selling gold at a fixed price should vary the price according to circumstances; thus a drain of gold could be prevented or restricted by raising the price of gold as well as the discount rate, and internal prices kept stable.

Experience in international cooperation for the maintenance of monetary stability may well lead in due course to still more fundamental changes than that of variation in the minimum reserve ratios of gold to notes. These may be the abolition of legal minimum ratios or even the abandonment of the gold standard. The value of a legal minimum ratio is much reduced now that gold no longer circulates within the country. The main purpose of the gold reserve is for adjusting international indebtedness, and there is no direct connection between this indebtedness and the total amount of the note issue. Yet the effect of keeping a minimum gold ratio is that this minimum is simply locked up and cannot be used in the settlement of international indebtedness. The only amount available for this purpose is the margin maintained above the legal minimum. Instead of relating note issue to gold reserve the volume of the note issue could be determined by experience at the amount required to maintain long-period stability of prices and the gold reserve at the amount found adequate by experience to settle international obligations. The reserve would, therefore, be determined according to the statistics of visible and invisible imports and exports, including the balance of capital and interest payments.

Faith in the gold standard is based mainly on the tradition for stability of value which it accidentally acquired during the nineteenth century and the early years of the present century. This was reinforced by monetary chaos of abandonment of the gold standard during the war and in immediately succeeding years. But these years were admittedly exceptional. In normal times, long-period stability of internal purchasing power could be maintained without the gold standard by coordinated control of currency in the different countries, while stability of the foreign exchanges could be effected by the use of short-term foreign assets to cover balances of international indebtedness. Such a system implies greater confidence and more cooperation between the nations than is found at present. However, these changes, i.e. abolition of the legal minimum ratios, and especially the abandonment of the gold standard, are too remote to merit detailed discussion here.

ORGANISATION OF INTERNATIONAL COOPERATION

Progress towards monetary stability may be made by informal cooperation between certain central banks on the lines practised during recent years. But the situation demands more systematic coordination of policy. This could be effected either by establishing special mechanism for the purpose or by using the already existing machinery of the League of Nations and the Bank for International Settlements.

Investigations by the League of Nations.

The League of Nations, through its Financial Committee, has played an important rôle in world financial reconstruction during the last decade. The problems of reconstruction were discussed by the International Financial and Economic Conferences organised by the League at Brussels in 1920 and at Genoa in 1922, and general principles were formulated for the guidance of

Governments and banking authorities in their efforts to restore stability to their financial systems. Also the League has taken a direct part in the financial reconstruction of Austria, Hungary, Greece, Bulgaria and Esthonia.

The Genoa Conference recognised that "measures of currency reform will be facilitated if the practice of continuous cooperation among central banks of issue, or banks regulating credit policy in the several countries, can be developed". Such cooperation would provide opportunities for coordination of policy. Credit would be regulated "not only with a view to maintaining the currencies at par with one another, but also with a view to preventing undue fluctuations in the purchasing power of gold".[1] For developing the necessary cooperation and coordination of policy the Conference recommended that "the Bank of England be requested to call a meeting of central banks as soon as possible to consider the proposals adopted by the Conference, and to make recommendations to their respective Governments for the adoption of an International Monetary Convention".[2]

The proposed meeting of central banks has not been convened, largely, no doubt, owing to the preoccupation of the various banks with internal problems of currency and finance. Thus there was the German

[1] The fluctuations of recent years could certainly be described as "undue".

[2] The quotations are respectively from Resolutions 3, 11, and 12, adopted by the Genoa Conference on the Report of its Financial Commission.

A detailed account of the implications of the Genoa Conference resolutions is given by R. G. Hawtrey in *The Gold Standard in Theory and Practice*, London, 1927.

collapse of 1923 and the restoration of stability in 1924, the British return to the gold standard in 1925, currency depreciations in France, Italy, Belgium, and Poland in 1926, followed by the establishment of relative stability in 1927 and 1928. Now, however, that these internal difficulties have been overcome, often by cooperation between central banks, the circumstances are more favourable for the development of systematic international coordination. As will be indicated later, this might well be effected in conjunction with the Bank for International Settlements.

During the years when the various countries were solving their internal currency problems, the Financial Committee of the League has given attention to the special problems of monetary stability discussed in this chapter. Thus the relation between monetary instability and unemployment was examined, on the initiative of the International Labour Organisation, by a joint committee of representatives of the Financial Committee and of experts appointed by the international Labour Office. This committee gave special attention to the relation between monetary policy and economic crises. In 1929 a further step was taken when the Financial Committee appointed the Delegation already mentioned above "to examine and report upon the causes of fluctuations in the purchasing power of gold and their effect on the economic life of the nations".[1] The Delegation has already held several

[1] League of Nations, Official Journal (Special Supplement No. 77), *Records of the Tenth Ordinary Session of the Assembly, Minutes of the Second Committee*, Geneva, 1929, p. 116. The delegation includes the heads of certain central banks and persons eminent in other branches of finance, together with several distinguished economists.

O

meetings and reached valuable tentative conclusions, some of which have been quoted in the present chapter.[1] Its work should provide the necessary preparation for effective cooperation and clearly much preparatory work is necessary on so complicated a subject.

Rôle of the Bank for International Settlements.

The Bank for International Settlements differs from the League of Nations in having a direct influence on monetary policy by its own financial power. How great this influence may become it is impossible to forecast at this early stage. It also offers opportunities for the development of close cooperation between central banks.

Its primary purpose is to act as agent for Reparation payments under the Young plan. In addition, however, its statutes provide that one of the objects of the Bank is "to promote the cooperation of central banks and to provide additional facilities for international financial operations".[2]

This cooperation will be facilitated by the frequent meetings of the Board of the Bank and by the work of its permanent international staff. It should become effective in the same way as the League of Nations system represents an advance towards world peace and cooperation over pre-war diplomatic methods with only occasional meetings of foreign Ministers and no permanent international staff to ensure adequate preparation and organisation. The statutes of the

[1] See also the *Second Interim Report of the Gold Delegation of the Financial Committee*, Geneva, 1931; this deals with the distribution of gold.
[2] Statutes of the Bank for International Settlements, Article 3.

Bank provide for its management by a Board which is to meet not less than ten times a year. The Board is composed of the Governors (or their nominees) of the central banks of Belgium, France, Germany, Great Britain and Italy, and nominees of United States and Japanese banking together with seven persons representative of finance, industry, or commerce appointed one each by the Governors or nominees of the banks, and not more than nine other persons elected from among lists of candidates submitted by the Governors or nominees of the banks. The Board may appoint advisory committees, chosen wholly or partly from persons not concerned with the Bank's management. The Statutes of the Bank aim at freedom of the management from political control and at ensuring that the operations of the Bank shall be in conformity with the monetary policy of the central banks of various countries.[1]

The regular and frequent meetings of representatives of the chief central banks in the management of the Bank for International Settlements must almost certainly lead to a coordination of monetary policy. Among the problems which will inevitably demand consideration is that of monetary stability; its solution

[1] With these objects in view the Statutes provide that:

(a) No person shall be appointed or hold office on the Board who is a member or an official of a Government, or is a member of a legislative body, unless he is the Governor of a central bank.

(b) Before any financial operation is carried out by or on behalf of the Bank on a given market or in a given currency the Bank shall afford to the central bank or central banks directly concerned an opportunity to dissent. In the event of disapproval being expressed within such reasonable time as the Board shall specify, the proposed operation shall not take place.

should be much facilitated by the opportunities for personal contacts and exchange of experience, information, and ideas which meetings of the Board will afford and by its systematic investigation by the Board's advisory committees. In addition to preparing the way for the central banks to reach international agreement on monetary stability, the Bank may make a direct contribution to economy in the use of the world's stock of monetary gold. Thus the central banks might regard their credit balances with the Bank as the equivalent of gold, the Bank might centralise and therefore economise part of the national gold reserves, while shipments of gold to meet temporary adverse balances may be avoided. Such developments will depend on the extent to which the central banks show increased confidence in one another and in the new Bank.[1] This in turn demands greater international confidence, security, and economic stability.

[1] The direct effects of the new Bank on the volume of credit and the level of prices throughout the gold-standard world are discussed by Mr. P. Barrett Whale in "Notes on the International Bank and the Creation of Credit". *Economica*, June 1930. Addresses and papers on the early operation of the Bank and its possibilities are given in the *Proceedings of the Academy of Political Science*, Vol. XIV, No. 2, January 1931, "The Young Plan in Operation", New York, 1931.

CHAPTER VIII

CONCLUSIONS

The forces of nationalism are seriously distorting the natural economic structure of the world. Natural economic boundaries do not coincide with national boundaries, and attempts to force them into the political framework involve economic loss by sacrificing the principle of efficiency, and put strain on international relations.

Before the developments of transportation and communications of the last hundred years, commerce and other economic relations were mainly localised, and, apart from trade in luxury goods, each State supplied almost all its own needs from within its own borders. Economic and political nationalism largely coincided. Progress in transportation has resulted in economic interests cutting across political boundaries, thus increasing international interdependence and strengthening the chances of maintaining the peace of the world. Resistance by nationalism to this development is a measure of the intensity of national rivalries and of insecurity and distrust.

The question is sometimes raised whether the causes of war are mainly political or mainly economic. It is not necessary to discuss this question here. It is, however, relevant to repeat that exaggerated nationalism, which seeks to identify the economic with the political, is now a great menace to world peace. Those who are endeavouring to prevent war should therefore include in their programme the diminution of economic armaments for the same reasons which impel them to propose measures for greater international security and reduction of naval, military, and air armaments.

In the present volume, four problems have been examined to illustrate the menace of economic nationalism and the injury inflicted by the barriers, conflict of policies, and lack of cooperation it involves. Protective tariffs are the most obvious of economic armaments, and being imposed by national legislatures represent close identity of economic with political nationalism. But many other weapons are forged by national Governments or by private organisations. They include direct and indirect subsidies, unfair methods of competition, unduly low wages and other conditions of labour. In monetary policy the piling up of exaggerated gold reserves in certain countries and the inadequacy of international cooperation have aggravated the world depression of trade. This in turn has strengthened the forces of economic nationalism and the demand for still greater economic armaments.

It is not denied that an industrial country may sometimes apply a policy of tariff protection with economic advantage. Tariff protection, or even prohibition of imports, may be justified where an important national industry is subjected to serious and unfair attack from abroad. But the value of tariff protection is very limited. Thus tariffs would not solve the British unemployment problem, since unemployment is greatest in the exporting industries. These industries are suffering from the growing industrialism of foreign countries, and the situation can be met effectively not by tariffs but by developing maximum efficiency in the old-established industries and by initiative in developing new industries. The gains of some industries from a system of scientific safeguarding tariffs would be small and would be more than off-set by injury inflicted on other industries and by the weakening of Britain's international leadership for greater liberty of trading. To secure international agreement for tariff reductions is admittedly difficult at present, owing to the force of vested interests entrenched behind high tariffs in many countries. Little progress is likely while the depression of trade persists, but a revival of prosperity and a growing sense of political security would facilitate reductions, especially in Europe.

Tariffs are unsatisfactory for dealing with intense international competition. The method is negative and is based on isolated national policy. More positive is the regulation of production and trade by international agreements. Large numbers of producers acting in isolation and often in ignorance of the trends of world demand are likely to cause successive waves of over-production and under-production. The amplitude of these waves would be reduced if estimates for each of the great staple commodities were made of probable world requirements in the early future and production adjusted to these requirements. The allocation of quotas of production to the different countries and to individual producers involves many difficulties, but would be superior to the present chaos of un-regulated competition which results in unfair practices and international bitterness.

Regulation of production would be more difficult in agriculture than in industry, because total output depends not only on the area under cultivation and the capital and labour applied but on the weather conditions which may result in a good or bad harvest. Where marketing is individual, producers are usually compelled to sell their output immediately, and this disturbs the world's economic system by causing wide fluctuations in prices. To meet this difficulty, regulation of the scale of production should be supplemented by Joseph's method in Egypt of creating a reserve or pool in the fat years to meet the shortage of the lean years.

The trends of world production and trade seem to be towards such kinds of organisation. International agreements on total production and on quotas, on allocation of markets or fixing of prices are increasing in number and importance. The development of international trusts should also tend towards a regulation of production. Up to the present the producers have been dominant in these agreements, while in many cartels the nationalist conception is retained. There is also the menace of monopoly, though some organisers of pools of surplus production and of agreements to restrict production have overreached themselves and involved their members in loss, instead of securing monopoly profits. Much progress is therefore necessary to establish agreements in industries engaged in specially severe competition, to increase the accuracy of estimates of future requirements of the market, and to safeguard the interests of consumers against the menace of producers' monopolies.

The use of low labour standards as a weapon in world competition results in bad industrial and international relations. Although it is true that a country's standards of labour conditions are determined mainly by its own productive efficiency and system of distribution, unfair wages and other low standards in any country undermine conditions abroad. International regulation of labour conditions is therefore desirable, and towards this end the International Labour Organisation has already achieved considerable progress. Little has, however, been done to deal with wages. The problems involved are admittedly very complicated, as it is difficult even to define "unfair" wages with precision. International investigations into wages, especially in industries suffering from severe competition, are necessary as a basis for agreements. A separate agreement for each industry would be required, and in view of the wide differences in wage standards in various countries, uniform minima would be quite impracticable; scales fixing ratios would, however, be feasible. Agreements on wages and other labour standards will be facilitated by agreements, on the lines indicated above, for the international regulation of production and trade.

Instability of monetary values, which is increased by conflict and lack of international cooperation in monetary policy, is responsible for an intensification of trade-cycle fluctuations. It is one of the important causes of the present depression. The recent great fall in the general level of wholesale prices has aggravated unemployment and increased the bitterness of international competition. This imposes strain both on industrial and international relations. Monetary instability, with its harmful consequences, will continue so long as the central banks pursue isolated policies with little regard for the effect on other countries. These policies result in monetary "armaments" which are the counterpart of tariffs, cut-throat trade competition, and unfair labour standards.

It is not recommended, as some propose, that Britain should abandon the gold standard. There are advantages in the countries of the world having the same basis for their monetary systems rather than a number of unrelated standards. But this increases the necessity for close cooperation, which should be directed to removing difficulties due to the present mal-distribution of the supplies of monetary gold. Cooperation is also needed in discount policy, while a modification by international agreement of the present ratios of gold reserves to note issues, together with other economies, may be necessary to meet the predicted world shortage of monetary gold. Progress along these lines is hoped from the investigations of the League of Nations and the operation of the Bank for International Settlements. It would provide a basis for greater stability in the economic system and thus reduce the insecurity and uncertainty upon which economic nationalism thrives.

Attempts during the last decade to secure reductions of economic armaments and to replace conflict by cooperation have been made difficult by exceptional economic chaos and political insecurity. National representatives in international conferences have manœuvred for agreements which would involve little or no modification of their own systems. Progress will be slow while this policy persists. But maximum welfare and prosperity cannot be enjoyed in narrow national compartments. A comprehensive programme of economic disarmament, based on recognition of the economic unity of the world, would increase the general prosperity of all peoples. It would make a contribution to world peace by widening the basis of human relationships and by preparing the foundations for a political system which would coordinate national with world citizenship.

INDEX